Governing in an Information Society

Steven A. Rosell et. al.

Institute for Research on Public Policy
Institut de recherche en politiques publiques

Printed in Canada

Legal Deposit Fourth Quarter
Bibliothèque nationale du Québec

Canadian Cataloguing in Publication Data

Main entry under title:

Governing in an Information Society

Foreword, preface and executive summary in English and
in French. Includes bibliographical references.

ISBN 0-88645-147-7

1. Information society—Government policy.
2. Information society—Government policy—Canada.
3. Canada—Politics and government—1984.
4. Political leadership. 5. International
organization. 6. Governmental investigations.
I. Rosell, Steven A. II. Institute for
Research on Public Policy.

JF1411.G68 1992   351'.000`   C92-090650-8

Institute for Research on Public Policy/
Institut de recherche en politiques publiques
Suite 200, 1470 Peel Street
Montreal, Quebec H3A 1T1

Cover artwork by Soren Henrich Design and Illustration
301-919 Fort Street, Victoria B.C. V8V 3K3

Table of Contents

FOREWORD

Too often, as we negiotiate the latest twists and intricacies of Canada's crisis of governance, we lose sight of the extent to which our experience is but one example of fundamental changes in governance occurring around the world. To some degree, as in other jurisdictions, we are trying to come to terms with global forces of transformation as they appear through the prism of our own history, culture, economic and political system. But those forces, and that context, are hard to see if we focus too much inwards, and backwards (in time), in efforts to deal with our own situation.

One of the most basic of those transformative forces is the emergence of a global information society. What are the implications for governance of the complex of social and technological changes that define the information society? What are more effective and appropriate ways of governing in that context? These are questions to which, as yet, research provides few answers. But they are questions with which practitioners increasingly must cope. To begin to address these issues more systematically, and to examine how they play through the crisis in governance we face, the IRPP convened a roundtable of researchers and government practitioners to undertake a two-year program of action research. This volume reports the first results of that program.

The report describes the ongoing process of learning undertaken by the participants which, itself, became a metaphor for the new approaches to governance the information society will require. With sometimes startling frankness, the participants draw on the insights of leading international authorities with whom they met, on case studies undertaken within their areas of responsibility, and on their own extensive experience, to question conventional ways of thinking, and to struggle toward a new understanding of governing in an information society. As they underline in this path-breaking report, they only could begin the work that will need to be done, but it is a most promising and thought-provoking beginning.

A number of the issues discussed in the report also are central to the new research agenda of the IRPP. They include strengthening our learning and educational capacity, rethinking our social contract, developing a shared framework for the development of regional Canadian economies in the new global context, and examining present and proposed Canadian institutions of governance in that same context. The report also demonstrates the value of finding innovative ways for researchers and practitioners to work together to address such issues, and that is an approach on which we should build.

Monique Jérôme-Forget
President
August 1992

AVANT-PROPOS

Il arrive trop souvent, alors que nous négocions les derniers détours du lacis complexe de la crise de la gouvernance au Canada, que nous perdions de vue l'importance du fait que notre expérience n'est qu'un des nombreux exemples des mutations radicales que la conduite des destinées de l'État connaît à travers le monde. D'une certaine manière, comme c'est le cas ailleurs, nous tentons de faire face aux courants de changement de nature planétaire, mais en les percevant à travers le prisme de l'histoire, de la culture, de l'économie et du régime politique qui sont les nôtres. Mais ces courants sont, tout comme leur contexte, difficiles d'appréhension dès lors que nous faisons preuve de trop d'introspection et de rétrospective en tentant de porter remède à notre propre cas.

L'un de ces vecteurs de mutation les plus immédiats est l'émergence d'une société planétaire de l'information. Quelles sont les répercussions, pour la gouvernance, des changements sociaux et technologiques complexes qui définissent la société de l'information? Et quels seraient, dans ce contexte, les modes de gouvernance plus efficaces et plus appropriés? Voilà autant de questions auxquelles la recherche n'apporte, pour l'instant, que peu de réponses, alors pourtant qu'elles interpellent de plus en plus les gouvernants. Soucieux d'examiner plus systématiquement ces contentieux et de déterminer leur interaction dans la crise de la gouvernance qui nous saisit, l'IRPP a réuni une table ronde de chercheurs et de décideurs gouvernementaux qui, pendant deux ans, allaient conduire un programme de recherches proactives. Le présent volume est le rapport des premiers résultats de cette initiative.

Ce rapport décrit l'inlassable effort d'apprentissage déployé par les participants, un processus qui devint en soi une métaphore pour désigner les nouvelles façons de concevoir la gouvernance rendues indispensables par la société de l'information. Avec une sincérité parfois déroutante, les participants se sont inspirés de la réflexion des sommités internationales qu'ils ont rencontrées à propos des études de cas dont elles s'étaient chargées dans leurs secteurs de compétence propres, mais également de leur vaste expérience personnelle, pour remettre en cause les raisonnements communément acceptés et tenter de longue lutte d'arriver à comprendre sous un jour nouveau la gouvernance dans une société de l'information. Comme ils le mettent en exergue dans ce rapport novateur, ils ne pouvaient que commencer la tâche qu'il faudra accomplir, mais c'est là un début prometteur et qui appelle à la réflexion.

Plusieurs des éléments abordés dans ce rapport sont également au coeur du nouveau programme de recherche de l'IRPP. Il s'agit entre autres de renforcer notre potentiel en matière d'apprentissage et d'éducation, de mettre en oeuvre un cadre commun en vue du développement des économies régionales au Canada dans le nouveau contexte planétaire, et de repenser, dans ce même contexte, les organes de gouvernance au Canada qui existent déjà et qu'on se propose d'implanter. Ce rapport prouve également l'intérêt qu'il y a de trouver, pour les chercheurs et les praticiens, de nouveaux moyens de travailler de concert pour trouver réponse à ce genre de questions, et c'est là un concept qu'il nous appartient d'exploiter.

Monique Jérôme-Forget
Présidente
Août 1992

vii

PREFACE

This report is the story of a work in progress. It describes the initial phase of an effort by a group of senior Canadian Public Servants, working with researchers and selected international authorities, to make sense of the implications for governance of the emergence of a global information society, and to develop more appropriate and effective approaches to governing in that new environment.

The idea for this project began to take shape while I was working with the International Development Research Centre, in a series of conversations with senior government officials and others involved in the governance process in several countries including Canada. What was striking about those discussions were the similarities in the dilemmas voiced, in the perceived crisis in governance described, even though those conversations were about very different political, economic and cultural systems. Many of those dilemmas seemed to have roots in the complex of social, economic and technological changes that has come to be called the "information society."

After I had moved to the Institute for Research on Public Policy (IRPP), we decided to test that idea by convening a meeting of senior Canadian government officials. In advance of that meeting, all participants received a brief discussion paper on the implications for governance of the information society, along with a number of relevant journal articles. The discussion that followed was quite remarkable, with participants recounting personal experiences of how the information society was changing the process of governance in their areas of responsibility, and beginning to explore some of the consequences of those changes.

The consensus at the end of the meeting was that these were fundamentally important issues that needed to be explored more systematically. At the same time, the participants noted that because these questions cut across departmental boundaries and exceeded the time horizon of most governmental planning, there was at present no place within government where such an inquiry could be carried on. There was a need, they concluded, to invent some new way to do that, and to do so in a way that also would bring to bear the insights and perspectives of those outside of government. This project became that invention.

The project was supported by more than a dozen Federal government departments and was organized as an experiment in participatory action research, in which the subjects of the research (the senior government practitioners in this case) themselves become an active part of the research team. While I coordinated the work of the project, and drafted the report, this is very much a collective effort in which the direction of the research, the design of case studies, the conclusions to be drawn and the content of the report all were determined by a roundtable of all participants. The members of that roundtable were:

Howard Balloch	Louise Frechette
Michael Binder	Roberto Gualtieri
Robert Blackburn	Jim Lahey
Anthony Campbell	Peter Liebel
Mel Cappe	Mary Murphy
Jeff Carruthers	Kathy O'Hara
Allan Darling	Morris Rosenberg
Mary Dawson	

They are very much co-authors of this effort, but final responsibility for what appears in the text and, in particular, for any errors or omissions, rests with me. In addition, during the life of the project, a number of roundtable members either left the government or were posted abroad, and so were unable to continue their participation. During their association with this effort, though, these former members of the roundtable contributed much to the work of the project:

Michael Bell	Ken Stein
Richard Dicerni	Richard Stursberg
John Paynter	Greg Traversy

Special mention should be made of the role played at the outset of the project by Allan Darling (then Deputy Secretary of the Treasury Board) and by Richard Stursberg (then Assistant Deputy Minister of Communications). Without their understanding and support it is unlikely that this path-breaking project could have been launched.

The substantive work of the project was supported by a secretariat composed of Arthur Cordell (senior advisor at the Department of Communications and a leading Canadian authority on the information society), James Taylor (Professor and Chairman of the Department of Communications at the Université de Montréal), and myself. In addition, Ian Stewart, formerly Deputy Minister of Finance, acted as a special advisor, participating in all roundtables and providing much insight, wisdom and thought-provoking comment throughout. Colleagues at the Meridian International Institute provided me with ongoing assistance and sound counsel throughout this effort.

The administrative support and organizational skills of Lynda Lennon, and later of Leigh McGowan, and the additional assistance provided by Melanie Burston kept this complex undertaking running smoothly against all odds. Lois Johnston looked after financial administration and also provided valuable editorial help in the preparation of the report.

Support and encouragement for the project throughout was provided by two successive Presidents of the IRPP. Rod Dobell was President of the Institute at the inception of the project and participated actively in roundtables during its first year. He was succeeded by Monique Jérôme-Forget, who continued to take an active part in the roundtables and to provide welcome support and encouragement.

The following pages describe the beginning of an effort by practitioners and researchers to understand how governance is changing in the information society, and what approaches would be more appropriate and effective in that new context. In the course of the project we began to see that governing in an information society involves a continuing process of learning, both within government and more broadly within society. The project itself can be seen as a microcosm of the sort of learning process required, a process that needs to be broadened to involve a wider range of participants. We hope that the publication of this initial report will be a step in that direction.

Steven A. Rosell
Coordinator
Project on Governing in
an Information Society

PRÉFACE

Le présent rapport relate l'histoire d'une oeuvre en cours de réalisation. Il décrit la phase initiale d'un effort accompli par un groupe de hauts fonctionnaires canadiens qui, de concert avec des chercheurs et un aréopage de sommités internationales, tentent de jeter le lumière sur les répercussions, pour la conduite des destinées de l'État, de l'émergence d'une société planétaire de l'information, et de définir des façons de gouverner plus appropriées et plus efficaces dans ce nouvel environnement.

L'idée de ce projet commença à germer alors que je travaillais avec le Centre de recherches pour le développement international, à l'occasion d'une série d'entretiens avec des hauts fonctionnaires et d'autres intervenants dans la conduite des affaires publiques de plusieurs pays dont le Canada. Lors de ces conversations, un élément frappant avait été le fait que les nombreux dilemmes ainsi évoqués, de même que la crise de la gouvernance qui semblait s'en dégager, présentaient bien des similitudes alors pourtant qu'il s'agissait de régimes politiques, de systèmes économiques et de cultures bien différents. Souvent, ces dilemmes semblaient avoir pris racine dans l'écheveau des mutations sociales, économiques et technologiques qui avaient fini par être baptisées du nom de "société de l'information".

Après mon arrivée à l'Institut de recherche en politiques publiques (IRPP), nous décidâmes de mettre cette idée au banc d'essai en réunissant des hauts fonctionnaires du gouvernement du Canada. Au préalable, tous les participants reçurent un document de discussion sommaire accompagné d'un certain nombre d'articles publiés dans des revues savantes au sujet des répercussions, pour la gouvernance, de la société de l'information. La discussion qui s'ensuivit fut assez remarquable, en ce sens que les participants y livrèrent les expériences qu'ils avaient vécues des multiples façons dont la société de l'information avait fait évoluer le mécanisme de la conduite des affaires publiques dans leurs secteurs de compétence propres, pour ensuite commencer à sonder certaines des conséquences de ces mutations.

A la fin de la réunion, les participants convinrent qu'il s'agissait là de questions d'une importance primordiale qui méritaient un examen plus systèmatique. Simultanément, ils constatèrent que, comme ces questions transcendaient largement les champs d'intervention individuels des ministères, ainsi que l'horizon chronologique des plans de l'État dans la plupart des cas, ce genre d'enquête systématique serait impossible à insérer dans l'infrastructure gouvernementale actuelle. Ils en conclurent qu'il fallait inventer le moyen d'en conduire une, mais également de le faire en y intégrant aussi les réflexions et les perspectives des milieux hors-gouvernement. Le projet devint le fruit de cette nécessité d'inventer.

Le projet reçut le concours de plus d'une douzaine de ministères fédéraux, et il fut orchestré comme une expérience de recherche proactive en coparticipation, en ce sens que les sujets de la recherche (en l'occurrence les hauts décideurs du gouvernement) devinrent eux-mêmes une composante active de l'équipe de recherche. Bien que j'aie personnellement assuré la coordination des activités ainsi que la rédaction du rapport, il s'agit essentiellement d'un effort collectif pour lequel l'orientation des recherches, la conception des études du cas, les conclusions à tirer et la teneur du rapport furent le produit d'une table ronde réunissant tous les participants, c'est-à-dire :

Howard Balloch	Louise Frechette
Michael Binder	Roberto Gualtieri
Robert Blackburn	Jim Lahey
Anthony Campbell	Peter Liebel
Mel Cappe	Mary Murphy
Jeff Carruthers	Kathy O'Hara
Allan Darling	Morris Rosenberg
Mary Dawson	

Ce sont essentiellement eux les co-auteurs de cette oeuvre, mais c'est sur moi que repose la responsabilité de ce que contient ce texte, et en particulier des erreurs ou omissions qui pourraient s'y être glissées. Qui plus est, au fur et à mesure que le projet se déroulait, certains participants quittèrent le gouvernement ou furent nommés à l'étranger, ce qui les empêcha de continuer à y participer. Toutefois, tant qu'ils furent du nombre, ces membres de la table ronde apportèrent beaucoup au projet :

Michael Bell	Ken Stein
Richard Dicerni	Richard Stursberg
John Paynter	Greg Traversy

Il convient en outre de souligner le rôle que joua d'emblée Allan Darling (alors sous-secrétaire au Conseil du Trésor), ainsi que celui de Richard Stursberg (alors sous-ministre adjoint des Communications). Sans leur compréhension et leur concours, il est peu probable que ce projet d'avant-garde eût pu voir le jour.

Le gros du travail entourant le projet bénéficia du concours d'un secrétariat composé d'Arthur Cordell (conseiller principal au ministère des Communications et qui fait autorité au Canada dans le domaine de la société de l'information), de James Taylor (professeur et président du Département des communications de l'Université de Montréal) et de moi-même. De plus, Ian Stewart, ancien sous-ministre des Finances, fit fonction de conseiller spécial, participant à toutes les réunions et faisant depuis le début profiter les participants de sa réflexion, de sa sagesse et de ses interventions toujours aptes à approfondir le débat. Mes collègues de l'Institut International Méridien m'ont apporté un concours de tous les instants et, pendant toute la réalisation du projet, m'ont été d'excellent conseil.

Le soutien administratif et les talents d'organisatrices de Lynda Lennon, puis de Leigh McGowan, ainsi que l'aide de Melanie Burston, ont permis, envers et contre tout, à cette entreprise complexe de se dérouler sans heurts. Lois Johnston assuma la gestion financière du projet et fut d'une aide précieuse lors de la mise en page du rapport.

Deux présidents successifs de l'IRPP offrirent pendant toute la durée du projet leur concours et leurs encouragements. Rod Dobell présidait l'Institut à la genèse du projet et, pendant la première année, il participa activement aux réunions de la table ronde. Il fut suivi par Monique Jérôme-Forget qui, à son tour, prit une part active aux travaux et offrit un concours et des encouragements très appréciés.

Les pages suivantes décrivent la genèse d'un effort déployé par des praticiens et des chercheurs pour mieux comprendre l'évolution de la gouvernance dans la société de l'information et déterminer les formules qui, dans cette conjoncture, seraient les plus appropriées et les plus efficaces. En conduisant ce projet, nous avons commencé à constater que l'art de gouverner dans une société de l'information faisait intervenir un phénomène d'apprentissage permanent, tant au sein du gouvernement que de la société au sens large. Le projet proprement dit peut être considéré comme un microcosme du genre de processus d'apprentissage ainsi rendu nécessaire, un processus qui doit être élargi de manière à y intégrer une plus grande palette de participants. Nous formulons l'espoir que la publication de ce premier rapport constituera un pas dans cette direction.

Steven A. Rosell
Coordonnateur
Projet sur l'art de gouverner
dans une société de l'information

Part I

Report of the Roundtable

Executive Summary

This report describes the initial findings of a roundtable of senior Canadian government officials, who have been working with researchers assembled by the Institute for Research on Public Policy (IRPP), to explore the implications for governance of the emergence of a global information society, and to develop more effective approaches to governing in that new context.

We are in the midst of a fundamental economic and social transformation whose extent and implications we only partially grasp. This transformation is being driven by an interplay of social and technological dynamics including, in particular:

- developments in information processing and telecommunications and the increasing links between those technologies;
- the emergence of a more educated and informed population and associated value changes;
- the increasing role and reach of the mass media;
- higher degrees of specialization in a more knowledge-based economy and consequent changes in the structure of work; and
- a much richer infrastructure of public and private organizations and a stronger degree of interaction amongst those organizations.

This transformation and the more richly interconnected, complex and turbulent world, the vast increase in information availability, and the compression in both time and space that result, has been labelled "the information society."

In this interconnected, turbulent environment, older ways of organizing and governing, which are premised on a more restricted flow of information and more limited interconnections (including public and corporate bureaucracies, and even representative democracy and the nation-state) seem to be overwhelmed. Initially, the roundtable focused on the disintegrative effects that the information society appears to have on established instruments and practices of governing, and on the crisis in governance that results. But gradually that focus shifted to a search for new ways of governing more appropriate to the realities of the information society.

Through discussions with international authorities, and case studies undertaken within the participating departments, the roundtable explored three basic themes:

- developing information-based ways of organizing within government;
- building consensus within the information society; and
- making more strategic use of information.

A principal result of that exploration was the realization that if we are to cope effectively with the environment of the information society, we will need to develop learning-based approaches to how we organize and govern ourselves. Effective leaders of such learning organizations or learning societies are those who take the lead in establishing an overall framework of goals, interpretations and values; and, in that context, give a wide range of players latitude to innovate and learn better ways to achieve those objectives.

What is becoming increasingly clear, as societies become more interconnected and as the number of players in the process of governance multiply, is that we need to invest more time and attention in developing a shared understanding of where we want to go, in a more systematic process of agenda-setting. Such a shared framework is the essential context that can allow the multiplying players in the governance process mutually to coordinate their actions. The development and continual evolution of that strategic framework, of that learning environment, is an essential part of effective governance and leadership in an information society.

The roundtable was able only to begin the exploration of approaches to governing called for by the new realities of the information society. Of the various issues and approaches detailed in the report, four were highlighted by the roundtable for special attention:

- constructing a shared framework and perspective across government;
- developing the Public Service as a learning organization;

- sharing knowledge as the key to effective leadership; and
- using information technology to foster societal learning.

At the same time, members of the roundtable recognized that there are many questions the project did not have the time or resources to address, and, no doubt, other questions that our current understanding of the information society did not yet equip us even to ask. In that light, the roundtable concluded that the success of the project should be judged by the extent to which it is not an end, but a beginning, the beginning of a more systematic search to develop new ways of governing appropriate to an information society. The roundtable only began to map this territory, began a process that needs to be continued with the involvement of a broader range of participants.

In microcosm, the project itself exemplifies the sort of learning effort required for effective governance in a turbulent environment. It was designed to bring together officials from a variety of departments to explore issues that transcend the boundaries of any single department and the usual time horizon of governmental planning and decision-making. It was designed to explore the changing context of governance and to begin to build a shared understanding, a shared framework, amongst the participants. Even more important, it was designed to foster a continuing process of constructing such frameworks, a continuing process of learning to make sense of and to cope with more turbulent environments.

The process of governing in an information society needs to be conceived as a process of learning both within the government and, more broadly, within society. A continuing reality of the information society will be that the lifespan of particular instruments of governing will be limited. To deal effectively with such a rapidly changing environment, we need to become far more effective at developing new ways of governing appropriate to new circumstances. This project has been one example, one beginning of the sort of ongoing learning process that will be required to underpin governing in an information society.

SYNTHÈSE

Ce rapport décrit les conclusions initiales d'une table ronde réunissant des hauts fonctionnaires du gouvernement du Canada qui, de concert avec des chercheurs appelés par l'Institut de recherches en politiques publiques (IRPP), ont examiné les répercussions, pour la conduite des affaires de l'État, de l'émergence d'une société de l'information à caractère planétaire, dans le but de définir des façons de gouverner plus efficaces dans ce nouveau contexte.

Nous vivons une époque de profondes mutations économiques et sociales, dont nous ne comprenons que partiellement l'envergure et les répercussions. Ces mutations sont animées par l'interaction des dynamiques sociales et technologiques, et notamment :

- les progrès réalisés dans les domaines du traitement de l'information et des télécommunications, ainsi que l'interaction de plus en plus marquée entre ces technologies;
- l'émergence d'une population de plus en plus instruite et davantage informée, et des nouvelles valeurs associées à ce phénomène;
- le rôle et la portée de plus en plus importants des médias de grande communication;
- l'hyperspécialisation dans une société davantage fondée sur la connaissance, et l'évolution corrélative de la structure du travail; et
- une infrastructure d'organismes privés et publics beaucoup plus riche, et un sens plus poussé de l'interaction entre eux.

Ces mutations, un monde beaucoup plus complexe et turbulent, où les liens sont devenus beaucoup plus étroits, une information beaucoup plus facilement accessible, ainsi que la compression spatio-temporelle qui l'accompagne, tout cela a été baptisé du nom de "société de l'information".

Dans cet environnement turbulent et étroitement interconnecté, les modes d'organisation et de gouvernement d'antan, qui reposaient sur un courant d'information davantage limité et sur des liens réciproques moins fournis (par exemple les bureaucraties des gouvernements et des entreprises, voire la démocratie parlementaire et l'État-nation) semblent dépassés. Dans un premier temps, la table ronde s'est penchée sur les effets désintégrateurs que la société de l'information semble avoir sur les appareils et les méthodes classiques de gouvernement, et sur la crise de la gouvernance qui en résulte. Mais petit à petit, l'attention des participants s'est mobilisée sur la recherche de nouveaux modes de gouvernance mieux adaptés aux réalités de la société de l'information.

Grâce à des entretiens avec des sommités internationales et des études de cas entreprises par les ministères participants, les membres de la table ronde ont étudié trois thèmes fondamentaux :

- l'élaboration, au gouvernement, de méthodes d'organisation reposant sur l'information;
- la formation d'un consensus au sein de la société de l'information; et
- une utilisation plus stratégique de l'information.

Cet examen minutieux eut pour résultat principal de faire constater que, pour pouvoir affronter plus efficacement l'environnement plus turbulent et davantage interconnecté créé par la société de l'information, il nous faut élaborer des méthodes basées sur l'acquisition des connaissances qui nous permettront de nous organiser et de nous gouverner. Les chefs de file avérés de ces organisations ou de ces sociétés ayant maîtrisé l'acquisition du savoir sont ceux qui ouvrent la voie en définissant un cadre général d'objectifs, d'interprétations et de valeurs et qui, dans ce contexte, donnent à une large gamme d'intervenants toute latitude pour innover et apprendre comment mieux atteindre ces objectifs.

Ce qui devient de plus en plus manifeste à mesure que les sociétés sont davantage reliées les unes aux autres et le nombre d'intervenants dans la gouvernance se multiplie, c'est qu'il nous faut consacrer davantage de temps et d'attention à faire connaître les objectifs que nous souhaitons atteindre en systématisant davantage les mécanismes d'élaboration des plans et des échéanciers. Cette vulgarisation est essentielle pour que les intervenants de plus en plus nombreux dans la gouvernance puissent mutuellement coordonner leur action. L'élaboration et l'évolution permanente de ce cadre stratégique, de cet environnement d'acquisition du savoir, sont les composantes obligées d'une gouvernance et d'un leadership efficaces dans une société de l'information.

Les membres de la table ronde n'ont pu que commencer seulement à examiner de près les modes de gouvernance qu'exigent les nouvelles réalités de la société de l'information. Au nombre des différents contentieux et démarches exposés en détail dans le rapport, les participants à la table ronde en ont fait ressortir quatre qui méritent une attention particulière :

- a mise en place, à l'échelle du gouvernement, d'un cadre et d'une perspective communs;
- la transformation de la fonction publique en une organisation d'acquisition du savoir;
- le partage des connaissances, élément indispensable à un leadership efficace; et
- l'utilisation de la technologie de l'information pour favoriser l'acquisition du savoir par la société.

Simultanément, les membres de la table ronde constatèrent que de nombreuses questions dépassaient les moyens mis à la disposition du projet ou l'envergure de son échéancier, et qu'indubitablement il s'en poserait d'autres qui transcendent encore notre entendement actuel de la société de l'information. Avec ce constat, la table ronde conclut que la réussite du projet ne pouvait être jugée que dans la mesure où celui-ci n'est pas une fin en soi, mais plutôt un commencement, le commencement d'une quête plus systématique de nouveaux modes de gouvernance mieux adaptés à une société de l'information. La table ronde n'a fait que commencer à jalonner cette terre encore vierge, en lançant une entreprise qui devra se poursuivre avec la participation d'une plus large palette d'intervenants.

Vu comme un microcosme, le projet exemplifie le genre d'effort nécessaire en fait d'acquisition du savoir pour obtenir une gouvernance efficace dans un environnement turbulent. Il a été conçu pour réunir des fonctionnaires de divers ministères afin qu'ils se penchent sur des questions qui transcendent les champs d'intervention de chacun de ces ministères de même que l'horizon chronologique habituel selon lequel les gouvernements tracent leurs plans et prennent leurs décisions. Il a également été conçu pour permettre un examen minutieux du contexte évolutif de la gouvernance et de jeter les bases d'un cadre et d'un entendement communs aux intervenants. Peut-être plus important encore, il a été conçu pour favoriser un mécanisme permanent d'édification pour ce genre de cadre, un mécanisme permanent d'acquisition du savoir permettant de comprendre et d'affronter des environnements sans cesse plus turbulents.

Le mécanisme de gouvernance dans une société de l'information doit être vu comme un processus d'acquisition du savoir, tant au sein du gouvernement que dans la société au sens large. L'une des réalités immuables de la société de l'information demeurera que la vie utile de tout appareil de gouvernance est limitée. Pour faire face efficacement à un environnement en mutation aussi rapide, il nous faut parvenir à mieux élaborer de nouvelles formes de gouvernance, mieux adaptées aux nouvelles conjonctures. Ce projet fut un exemple, le commencement de ce genre de processus permanent d'acquisition du savoir qui deviendra indispensable pour gouverner dans une société de l'information.

1

Introduction

We are in the midst of a fundamental economic and social transformation whose extent and implications we only partially grasp.
This transformation is being driven by an interplay of social and
technological dynamics including, in particular:

- developments in information processing and telecommunications
  and the increasing links between those technologies;
- the emergence of a more educated and informed population and
  associated value changes;
- the increasing role and reach of the mass media;
- higher degrees of specialization in a more knowledge-based
  economy and consequent changes in the structure of work; and
- a much richer infrastructure of public and private organizations
  and a stronger degree of interaction amongst those organizations.

This transformation and the more richly interconnected, complex
and turbulent world, the vast increase in information availability,
and the compression in both time and space that result, has been
labelled "the information society."[1] While much of the research
and discussion of the information society to date has focused on its
effects on industry, markets and the economy, the implications of
the information society for governance are at least as significant.

---

[1] See, for example: Bell, D., "The Social Framework of the Information Society," in T.
Forester(ed) *The Microelectronics Revolution* (Oxford: Basil Blackwell, 1980); Cleveland,
H., "The Twilight of Hierarchy: Speculations on the Global Information Society." *Public
Administration Review* (January/February 1985); Conklin, D. and Deschênes (eds) *Canada's
Information Revolution* (Ottawa: Supply and Services Canada, 1991); Cordell, A., *The
Uneasy Eighties: The Transition to an Information Society* (Ottawa: Science Council of
Canada, 1985); Diebold, J., *Business in the Age of Information* (New York: Amacom,
1985); Dizard, W.P., *The Coming Information Age* (New York: Longman, 1982); Gotlieb,

Research and analysis of the changes in governance being wrought by the information society are still at an early stage, but practitioners, of necessity, have been developing innovative approaches to deal with the new realities. For this reason the insights and experience of practitioners are likely to be at least as important as those of researchers in finding practical and effective approaches to governing in the information society. What has been lacking is a mechanism to allow those practitioners to learn about relevant innovations that are being tried elsewhere and in the absence of such a mechanism, too often the wheel is reinvented and mistakes are repeated. As well, with the daily pressure of events, practitioners generally have too little time to reflect on their own innovations and to learn from that experience.

The Design of the Project: Participatory Action Research

To remedy that, and to begin a more systematic investigation of the implications of the information society for the process of governance, the Institute for Research on Public Policy (IRPP) invited a group of senior Canadian government officials to come together in what was called the Governing in an Information Society Roundtable. The project was designed as an experimental program of *participatory action research* (PAR)* in which the participants would be the authors of a process that, over the course of two years, would involve practitioners, researchers and others from within and outside government. Participatory action research:

C.C. (ed), *The Information Economy: Its Implications for Canada's Industrial Strategy* (Ottawa: The Royal Society of Canada, 1984); Michael, D.M., "Too Much of a Good Thing? Dilemmas of an Information Society," *Technological Forecasting and Social Change* (Vol. 25, 347-354, 1984); Nora, S. and Minc, A., *L'informatisation de la societé* (Paris: Le Seuil, 1978); Porat, M.U., *The Information Economy* (Washington: Dept. of Commerce, 1977); Schon, D.A., *Beyond the Stable State* (New York: Norton, 1973); and the various issues of the journal *The Information Society.*

... is oriented in principle towards the active involvement of the subjects of research in the identification of the research topic, in planning and implementing field work, in sharing in the analysis process, and in deciding upon and initiating actions derived from newly acquired information or knowledge. .... In effect the research*ed* (those who must deal with or resolve the issues under study) become themselves the research*ers*.[2]

This project involved senior officials from more than a dozen government departments, and researchers drawn together by the IRPP, in a two-year exploration of the implications for governance of the emergence of a global information society. The project proceeded at two levels:

* roundtable discussions with leading Canadian and international authorities on broad questions related to governance in the information society; and
* case studies undertaken by the senior officials to reconsider (in the context of the project) specific issues within their own areas of departmental responsibility, the results of which also were reported to the roundtable.

---

[2] MacLure and Loevinsohn, *Participatory Research in IDRC* (Ottawa: IDRC, 1988).

* PAR is an active, collaborative form of inquiry involving both researchers and practitioners in a manner that is quite different from more traditional models of research. As the *American Behavioral Scientist*, in a recent issue devoted to PAR, put it:

Participatory action research thus contrasts sharply with the conventional model of pure research in which members of organizations and communities are treated as passive subjects, with some of them participating only to the extent of authorizing the project, being its subjects, and receiving the results. PAR is applied research, but it also contrasts sharply with the most common type of applied research in which researchers serve as professional experts, designing the project, gathering the data, interpreting the findings, and recommending action to the client organizations. .... In PAR some of the members of the organizations we study are actively engaged in the quest for information and ideas to guide their future actions.

The article went on to outline some of the benefits to practitioners of involvement in PAR, noting in particular:

The way we think about problems is shaped to a considerable extent by the social setting in which we find ourselves. When we are at work the organization provides

In the course of the project, the roundtable met 14 times, heard 11 presentations by outside authorities and reviewed the results of 12 departmental case studies. Roundtable members also received regular summaries of relevant books and articles, which were circulated both by electronic mail (on the government's Senior Executive Network) and in hard copy. During the project, the roundtable defined its own course through periodic agenda-setting sessions at which lessons learned to date were reviewed and used as the basis to define the subject-matter for future roundtables. At those sessions the progress of the departmental case studies also was reviewed, allowing participants mutually to coordinate their studies, and to provide suggestions on the cases being undertaken by others.

After each roundtable (whether outside authorities were involved or case studies were reviewed) the secretariat provided participants with a summary record of discussion. The summaries were not transcripts, but rather provided the gist of key ideas and exchanges from those sessions. Participants then were asked to confirm the substantive accuracy and completeness of the summmaries. The focused feedback provided by those summaries was an essential aid to the learning process of the roundtable, and provided a

---

that setting. We think and act within organizational structures and cultures that provide explicit and implicit ground rules determining what information and ideas are relevant for problem solving. . . . In situations of major social change, the prevailing ground rules are likely to block the path to creative solutions of serious new problems.

One of the benefits for practitioners of involvement in PAR, in this view, is that of being able to step outside the usual organizational context, to examine major questions afresh, in a different context. The article goes on as well to note a major benefit for researchers:

Practitioners often bring the pursuit of irrelevant or ill-conceived lines of inquiry to a rapid halt, correcting or defining the questions asked in ways that lead to sharper formulation and more productive research. . . . Active involvement with practitioners struggling to solve important practical problems is highly likely to open up researchers' minds to new information and new ideas, leading to advances in theory as well as in practice.

(The last three quotations are taken from Whyte, W.F., Greenwood, D. and Lazes, P., "Participatory Action Research for Science and Society," *American Behavioral Scientist* (1989).)

valuable chronicle of that process. Throughout this report we will make frequent use of quotes from the summaries.

The project was not conceived primarily as a problem-solving exercise, but rather as a way to explore how the process of governance is changing in the information society, and to begin to redefine the problems of governance in that context. From the beginning it has been clear that we could only hope to begin this process. Therefore, our purpose has been to map the territory, to identify promising lines for future development, and to test the extent to which an inquiry of this sort can help to develop more effective ways to understand and to deal with the crisis in governance we now face.

A Crisis of Governance

We began the project with the sense that there is a crisis facing systems of governance around the world, including Canada. Statements expressing that concern recurred throughout the project. As one participant put it:

> I keep coming back to the issue that if we were in a private-sector organization in today's environment, with all of the pressures of change, globalization, and international competitiveness, we would be stepping back and looking at our structure. We would be asking ourselves can we live with that? (In our case, can we live with the behemoth that is the Federal government?) The answer would be 'no way!' And we also would be looking at our judicial and parliamentary systems, listening to some of the concerns being expressed by people, watching what's happening in Europe and asking ourselves whether the institutions that we currently have are suited to dealing with the kinds of changes that are taking place today? And again I think the answer would be no. . . .
>
> And, I guess, the issue is: do we take the structure we currently have and try to fine-tune it, which is the traditional way of doing things, or somehow do we start saying to ourselves, more fundamentally, is this the way we want it? . . . To me this is an issue that no one wants to deal with but, I guess, in a sense, it's staring us in the face. . . .

As we will see in the following chapters, we heard a variety of cases in which the traditional apparatus of government seemed less and less capable of effective response to new challenges, so that in the end, the only way to generate any response was to bypass the apparatus. As one group of participants phrased it in a report to the roundtable: "... in a crisis, the system essentially abandoned the system."

We also heard the depressingly familiar statistics on loss of public confidence in government, on the diminishing legitimacy of the system. Nor, it was pointed out, was this loss of legitimacy and confidence limited to Canada. We can see examples of this almost everywhere we look, including striking examples of upheavals in governance in Europe and in the developing world.

We recognized that many factors, in addition to the entry into an information society, contributed to that crisis in governance. But a persuasive case was made to us by a wide variety of invited experts—and was reinforced further by case studies undertaken in our own areas of responsibility—that many of the roots of the current crisis are to be found in new patterns of human interconnection, which are closely coupled to the emergence of a new information and communications environment. The more important changes are occurring below the surface and engender a transformation of the very ground rules of governance. In the project we sought to explore the extent to which the information society is generating that crisis in governance, to interpret the crisis through the lens of the information society, and to see whether that perspective might suggest more effective and appropriate approaches to governing in this new environment.

We were influenced in our early discussions by a seminal article by Harlan Cleveland,[3] who has been leading an international project to rethink global governance in the context of the information society, and who was formerly U.S. Assistant Secretary of State, Ambassador to NATO and Dean of the Hubert Humphrey Institute of Public Affairs. In that article he linked the crisis in governance worldwide to the "informatization of society," and to a resulting fundamental shift in the basic organizing principle of society:

---

[3] Cleveland, op. cit.

Knowledge is power, as Francis Bacon wrote in 1597. So the wider the spread of knowledge, the more power gets diffused. For the most part individuals and corporations and governments don't have a choice about this. . . .

Once information can be spread fast and wide—rapidly collected and analyzed, instantly communicated, readily understood by millions—the power monopolies that closely held knowledge used to make possible were subject to accelerating erosion.

In the old days when only a few people were well educated and 'in the know,' leadership of the uninformed was likely to be organized in vertical structures of command and control. Leadership of the informed is different: it results in the necessary action only if exercised mainly by persuasion, bringing into consultation those who are going to have to do something to make the decision a decision. . . .

In an information-rich polity, the very definition of 'control' changes. Very large numbers of people empowered by knowledge—coming together in parties, unions, factions, lobbies, interest-groups, neighborhoods, families, and hundreds of other structures—assert the right or feel the obligation to 'make policy.'

Decision making proceeds not by 'recommendations up, orders down,' but by development of a shared sense of direction among those who must form the parade if there is going to be a parade. . . .

'Planning' cannot be done by a few leaders, or by even the brightest whiz-kids immured in a systems analysis unit or a planning staff. Real-life 'planning' is the dynamic improvisation by the many on a general sense of direction—announced by the few, but only after genuine consultation with those who will have to improvise on it.

According to Cleveland, this new information environment, and the diffusion of power that results, is having dramatic effects on governance and, in particular, on the nation-state:

> . . . power is leaking out of sovereign national governments in three directions at once.

> The State is leaking at the top, as more international functions require the pooling of sovereignty in alliances, in a World Weather Watch, in

geophysical research, in eradicating contagious diseases, in satellite communication, in facing up to global environmental risks.

The State is leaking sideways, as multinational corporations—'private,' pseudoprivate, and 'public'—conduct more and more of the world's commerce, and operate across political frontiers so much better than committees of sovereign states seem able to do.

The State is also leaking from the bottom, as minorities, single-issue constituencies, special-purpose communities and neighborhoods take control of their own destinies, legislating their own growth policies, their own population policies, their own environmental policies.

Cleveland's argument reiterated for us that the crisis in governance that we are experiencing is in no way unique to Canada. As one roundtable member put it: "The fault lines may depend on our particular history and circumstances, on 1759 and all that, but the reasons we are having an earthquake has more to do with the forces that are triggering earthquakes in Europe, the developing world and almost everywhere we look." Another added (this was in 1989) "Yes, Gorbachev, too, is riding the information tiger."

At our initial meetings, we tried to identify the most prevalent manifestations, or effects relevant to governance, of what Harlan Cleveland had called the informatization of society. These included:

- *The trend to globalization:* including the globalization of the economy (interconnected stock exchanges, frontierless capital markets, globalization of manufacturing and so on), the pervasive influence of globalized science and technology, and the growing requirement to handle issues, from trade to the environment to human rights and more, in supranational fora, networks and organizations.

- *Atomization, democratization, and fragmentation:* reflected in the increasing power of sub-national governments, in growing regionalism, and in the proliferation of "multiple voices," that is, the increase in the number and influence of groups organizing to assert a role in the process of governance.

- *A breakdown of the bureaucratic / industrial model of organizing:* both public and private sectors are downsizing, stripping away middle management, contracting out work (and in the public sector, privatizing functions), and relying more on networks and task forces and other more flexible, decentralized ways of organizing.

- *Human resources* are increasingly the key asset in both the public and private sectors.

- *A fundamental restructuring:* the breakdown of the historical distinctions between industries, between the public and private sectors and even between states, accompanied by a search for new relationships and alliances between those entities.

- *The decreasing possibility of secrecy,* and the implications of that for governing systems that rely on a certain degree of confidentiality.

New Conceptual Lenses

But even as we did this we were keenly aware of the inadequacy of our own conceptual frames. As Harlan Cleveland had warned in the article cited earlier:

> The historically sudden dominance of the information resource has, it seems to me, produced a kind of theory crisis, a sudden sense of having run out of basic assumptions. ... somewhere near the center of the confusion is the trouble we make for ourselves by carrying over into our thinking about information (which is to say symbols) concepts developed for the management of things—concepts such as property, depletion, depreciation, monopoly, 'inevitable' unfairness, geopolitics, the class struggle, and top-down leadership.

Cleveland went on to describe some of the ways in which information differed from material resources, differences that would require a basic rethinking of many concepts we take for granted:

1. *Information is expandable* . . . It expands as it is used.
2. *Information is not resource hungry.* . . . . . . the production and distribution of information are remarkably sparing in their requirements for energy and other physical and biological resources.
3. *Information is substitutable.* It can and increasingly does replace capital, labour and physical materials.
4. *Information is transportable*—at close to the speed of light.
5. *Information is diffusive.* It tends to leak. . . . . . . the leakage of information is wholesale, pervasive, and continuous. . . . . . . monopolizing information is very nearly a contradiction in terms.
6. *Information is shareable.* . . . if I sell you my automobile, you have it and I don't. But if I sell you an idea or give you a fact, we both have it.

So from the outset of the project we had a sense that our traditional conceptual frames actually could blind us to much that is important about the information society and its implications for governance. As one member put it at an early roundtable:

> The danger is that we would just be reinforcing our own ignorance. We need to be open to outside resource people, to let them tell us what they think is important. We should not focus too soon. It is too early to come down to specifics. We need to explore more broadly. We should start with people who will really open up our thinking.

That recognition also underlined the value of using the PAR model for the project, so that we could explore this territory in a more open way. It also led us to invite Harlan Cleveland to be the guest expert at one of our first roundtables, so that he could help in our early efforts to develop some conceptual lenses through which we might better be able to perceive the implications of the information society. We also met early in the project with Donald Michael, one of the deans of technological forecasting and a seminal thinker in this field. The next few pages outline some of the conceptual frames that arose out of those conversations, as well as in other discussions and research.

Defining some Terms

From the outset of the project our focus was not just on "government" but on "governance." *Governance* derives from the Greek "kyberman" and "kybernetes" which mean "to steer" and "pilot or helmsman" respectively (the same Greek root from which "cybernetics" is derived). The process of governance is the process whereby an organization or society steers itself, and the dynamics of communication and control are central to that process. While the role of government is and remains central to the process of governance, in the information society more and more players—voluntary organizations, interest groups, the private sector, the media and so on—become involved in that process.

Harlan Cleveland, in his presentation to the roundtable, provided a valuable way of conceptualizing *information,* which we used throughout the project:

> One important piece of vocabulary that it would be worth trying to get straight is the distinction between data, information, [and] knowledge. . . . Let me suggest one way of thinking about it that I find helpful:
>
> *data* are unrefined ore, undifferentiated facts without contexts;
>
> *information* is refined ore, organized data, but data which we have not yet internalized (it is the newspapers we have not yet read, the course we have not yet taken);
>
> *knowledge* is information which we have internalized, information which we have integrated with our own internal frameworks. It is information integrated by me and is therefore personal and pluralistic. Information is general, knowledge is personal. Information can be held in common, knowledge cannot. . . .

As we shall see later in this report, Cleveland's distinctions amongst data, information and knowledge became important parts of the vocabulary of the project. In particular, it helped us to see that the process of translating data and information into knowledge (the process by which data and information are interpreted, given meaning and so made useful as a basis for action) is central to effective governance in an information society.

A more Interconnected Society

While the term "information society" often conjures images of the technologies that clearly have been central to its emergence, for us the hallmark of the information society is the growing degree of interconnection that is emerging, both within the state and across national boundaries. This is fundamental to the challenge posed by the information society for governance.

As society becomes more interconnected, what we are faced with is a *loss of boundaries*. Obvious examples include changing political boundaries, including the rise of regional trading areas, and loss of boundaries between industries. But boundaries are fundamental to identity, to organization and to governance. So we find ourselves engaged in a continual process of trying to redefine those boundaries. For example, as globalization makes nation-state boundaries less salient, we see populations around the world trying to reorganize themselves around more natural economic or ethnic boundaries. Globalization and regional fragmentation can be seen as parts of the same process of restructuring.

The loss of boundaries we are experiencing also throws into question basic conceptual distinctions that we use to make sense of the world. Harlan Cleveland, in his presentation to the roundtable, cited as examples the longstanding distinctions between goods and services, and between the public and private sectors:

> Cray computer, defines the machines it produces as being composed of a large amount of knowledge and a small amount of sand. It is instructive to think about goods and services in that way. The concepts of economics, and the distinction it makes for example between goods and services, are decreasingly helpful. For example, the French economist, Albert Bressand, uses the case of a McDonald's hamburger: it consists of some wheat and meat but that is the smallest part of the cost of production. Far more important are the highly developed procedures and process for production and for service. Bressand then asks should the McDonald's hamburger be considered a good or a service, and concludes that it is not an important question. In the information economy what we are dealing with instead are complex packages of goods and services (which Bressand calls 'compax').

Government has great difficulty in catching up with this sort of fundamental shift in thinking. For example, it is increasingly difficult to estimate the percentage of information workers in society. Most goods have an increasing ratio of information or knowledge content. It does not help to count as a manufacturer a white-collar worker whose job is to operate a robot. We therefore face an enormous conceptual and vocabulary problem. . . .

Another conceptual distinction that is changing in the information society (another vocabulary problem) is that between the public and the private. In the face of privatization, alliances between government and industry, contracting out and the like, the distinction between public and private is being blurred. And that blur is where the action is, where the most interesting developments in society and governance are happening. . . .

Increasingly we need to look at governance as a combination of public and private sector activities, and at the building of such public-private partnerships as the most dynamic aspect of systems of governance.

Donald Michael, in an article circulated to participants before his presentation to the roundtable,[4] took this a step further, arguing that our traditional conceptual apparatus no longer is adequate for dealing with this interconnected world:

It is the values held by a person, organization, and society that determine what information is important, what interpretations are useful. Indeed, values define what constitutes a 'problem' or 'opportunity' and a way of dealing with it. . . .

Currently we lack a shared set of values that interprets the world and acts toward it as a *systemic* world; that is, as interconnected and interdependent at all levels. We face an unprecedented state of practical affairs: a world where information is rapidly creating a situation where everything is connected with everything else. . . . Few of us, professionals or lay citizens, are skilled in thinking in systemic terms. . . .

Again, we found that we were exploring a territory for which there is no reliable map. This inadequacy of our conceptual apparatus to make sense of proliferating information usually is

---

[4] Michael, D.N., "The Search for Values in the Information Age," *Western City* Vol. LXIV, No. 9 (1988).

described and experienced as information overload. But as our exploration continued, it seemed more useful (and productive of solutions) to see the real problem as the insufficient capacity of our existing frameworks and methods of interpretation to translate that data and information into meaningful knowledge (to use the vocabulary suggested by Harlan Cleveland). The blossoming of the information economy can be seen, in the same context, as arising from the burgeoning demand to find better ways to interpret: to translate data and information into knowledge.

The Law of Requisite Variety

The inadequacy of existing conceptual frames to make sense of a more interconnected society, has a parallel in the inadequacy of more traditional ways of organizing to cope with a more interconnected society. This is not surprising given the tight coupling between how we think and how we organize, between communication and control. As society becomes more inter-connected, older ways of organizing and governing (which are premised on the ability to limit and channel flows of information) break down. In the past, the notion that "everything is connected to everything else" has had to be dismissed, since the resulting situation would be unmanageable. But at present that coping strategy is being overwhelmed and the result is recurring crisis.

Late in the project we encountered one theoretically powerful way to understand this: the Law of Requisite Variety, which comes from cybernetics, the science of information and control.[5] That law states that the variety of the regulator (essentially the number of different configurations it can assume or process) needs to be in some sense comparable to the variety of the system being regulated. (More formally, it states: "R's capacity as a regulator cannot exceed

---

[5] The original statement of the Law of Requisite Variety can be found in Ashby, W.R., *Introduction to Cybernetics* (New York: Wiley, 1956).

R's capacity as a channel of communication.")When that is not the case, the capacity of that regulator (its capacity for communication and control) is overwhelmed.

In the context of the information society, we might say that as society becomes more complex and interconnected, and so takes on more variety, more possible configurations, the capacity of existing regulatory (governance) systems is being overwhelmed. When this happens, there are essentially two alternatives: increase the variety of the regulator or reduce the variety of the system being regulated.

Bureaucracy and many traditional instruments of governance deal with the situation primarily by trying to reduce the variety of the regulated system by attempting to restrict the flow of information (using hierarchy as a filtering mechanism, through routinized procedures, secrecy and so on). There is an extensive literature on bureaucratic forms of organization that documents and elaborates these characteristics.[6] One frequent strategy is to seek to separate policy and implementation, relying on a planning group to support decision-makers in devising an elaborate blueprint, weighing "all" of the relevant factors and options, and then handing the result to others to implement. The effect is to attempt to reduce the variety of the system to the information-handling capacity of the planning group and decision-makers. But as the information revolution unfolds, as the environment becomes more interconnected, turbulent and unpredictable, that approach is becoming less and less sustainable.

---

[6]This literature is very extensive. See, for example, Beniger, J.R., *The Control Revolution* (Cambridge: Harvard University Press, 1986); Crozier, M., *Le phénomène bureaucratique* (Paris: Editions du Seuil, 1963); Katz, D, and Kahn, R.L., *The Social Psychology of Organizations* (New York: Wiley, 1966); March, J.G., and Simon, H.A., *Organizations* (New York: Wiley, 1958); Merton, R.K. "Bureaucratic Structure and Personality," *Social Forces*, 1940: 560-568; Thompson, J.D., *Organizations in Action* (New York: McGraw Hill, 1967); Weber, Max, *The Theory of Social and Economic Organization* (New York: The Free Press, 1964). Also relevant is the growing literature in economics that argues that as information technology lowers transaction costs, markets become more efficient than hierarchies as ways of organizing activity. See, for example, Wlliamson, O., *Markets and Hierarchies* (New York: The Free Press, 1975).

Leadership in the Information Society

The project became, in effect, a search for ways to increase the variety and capacity of the regulating (governing) system, a search to understand what constitutes effective leadership in the information society. As the following chapters will detail, we came to see that increasing the capacity of the governing system meant developing learning approaches to how we organize and govern ourselves. The growing reliance on networks and markets is a part of that (one example of a learning approach), but only a part. In the information society, the governance system needs to include a wider range of players, in addition to government. To be effective in that expanded governance system, government needs to "learn to" operate at a higher level, managing the ways in which issues are framed and the process by which they are addressed.

In this view, leadership in the information society, whether in organizations or society more broadly, involves taking the lead in establishing that framework, establishing a common set of goals, interpretations and values, a shared vision, and within that context providing a wide range of players with wide latitude to experiment, innovate and learn better ways to achieve those objectives. A seminal article in the organizational literature provides a strikingly parallel statement of this proposition.[7]

That article seeks to establish the form of leadership that is required as the environment becomes more turbulent and interconnected. It postulates four ideal types of environment, ranged along a continuum from least to most interconnected. It begins with what is called a "placid randomized environment" which corresponds to the economist's classical market and is composed of many small, separate units very loosely connected. At this level there is no distinction between strategy and tactics in the type of leadership required. The next type of environment is termed "placid-clustered" and is like the economist's imperfect competition, characterized by larger units in tighter interaction. The environment becomes more patterned and survival depends on

---

[7] Emery, F.E. and Trist, E.L., "The Causal Texture of Organizational Environments," *Human Relations* (18) 1965: 21-32.

what an organization knows of that environment. As a result, strategy becomes differentiated from tactics.

Further along the continuum is the "disturbed-reactive" environment, which is like the economist's oligopolistic market. Here many large units of the same type interact and must take each others' actions into account. To do this, a new function is added between strategy and tactics called operations—a military term having to do with drawing off opponents (bluffing, collusion, etc.). The final, most interconnected type of environment is called the "turbulent field." The authors state that: "... the dynamic properties arise not simply from the interactions of the component organizations, but also from the field itself. The ground is in motion." The organizations have become so richly interconnected that the effect is like that of soldiers marching in step over a bridge. To cope with this situation, the authors argue, requires leadership that focuses at the level of "... values that have overriding significance for all members of the field."

As society becomes more interconnected, as we reach the level described in the article as a turbulent field and that we characterized earlier as loss of boundaries, the appropriate form of leadership is one that operates at the level of values, of constructing a shared vision and framework of interpretation in the context of which an organization or society learns and adapts. Much of this report will focus on our exploration of different ways of accomplishing that.

The Shape of the Report

Early in our discussions we defined three basic themes around which to organize our work. The first was to examine the implications of the information society for organizing within government. Second, we wanted to focus on the process of building consensus more broadly within the information society. And, third, we were interested in exploring the techniques of handling information that seemed to underpin both the process of organizing and the ways of building consensus in this new environment.

At first we tended to be preoccupied with the ways in which the "informatization of society" had a disintegrative effect on existing ways of organizing and governing. But as our discussions progressed, our focus shifted to a search for more effective ways of organizing and governing, given the realities of the information society. As a progress report prepared at the mid-point of the project noted:

> . . . while initially we may have tended to focus on the theme of disintegration, we have subsequently begun to see the issue as being one of *new ways of integrating.* . . . *integrative mechanisms based on the principle of hierarchical, or vertically structured, systems of decision-making and control, with all that is thereby implied in restrictions on communication, tend to experience considerable difficulties in an era of abundant, undifferentiated and marketable information flows.* . . .we may now want to revise our earlier assumption that signs of fragmentation are simply indices of disintegration, and instead see the matter as a challenge for the development of more horizontally structured mechanisms of integration.
>
> The problem then becomes one of the *transition from one system of integration*, strongly vertical in its tendency, *to another*, with its greater emphasis on horizontal patterns of arriving at decision-making and policy-formulation.

The next three chapters tell the story of our search for such new ways of integrating. Each chapter deals with one of the three themes around which we organized our work throughout the project :

- the development of more information-based ways of organizing within government (Chapter 2);
- consensus-building in an information society (Chapter 3);
- how to make more strategic use of information (Chapter 4).

In Chapter 5 we draw together the preliminary conclusions we have reached in this exploration.

2

Information-based Ways of Organizing

At the outset of its work, the roundtable conceptualized the issue of information-based ways of organizing in the following way:

> Similar to trends in industry, government is running up against the limitations of the bureaucratic/industrial model of organizing, and is exploring ways to develop more flexible, rapid response mechanisms that can mobilize a wider range of resources; and at the same time seeking to reduce its own size, strip away levels of management, rely more on networks and task forces, and farm out (privatize or contract out) a variety of functions previously done in-house.
>
> Increasingly the boundaries between organizations and departments are being called into question as issues become more interconnected and as the key to success becomes finding ways to pull together resources needed to address a given issue from a variety of departments and organizations. Within organizations that are becoming more knowledge-based, there also are fundamental changes taking place in work structure, in part as a result of greater use of information technology and increasing specialization.
>
> Overall, more and more emphasis is being given to the development of less hierarchical, more flexible forms of organizing, both within and amongst organizations. While the private sector, spurred by the requirements of competitiveness, appears to be well ahead in this exploration, the public sector increasingly is following a parallel road, driven in part by fiscal stringency coupled with growing public demands for more effective and responsive service. To what extent can and should the public sector adopt the newer, information-based ways of organizing that increasingly are common in the private sector. How can we develop more 'nimble' public-sector organizations?

This chapter outlines what the roundtable has learned in exploring these questions and highlights the ideas and issues that we believe merit further attention. The roundtable was structured to encourage exploration and open-ended inquiry, not to reach final recommendations. Nevertheless, certain themes recurred throughout the process providing an increasingly clear image of the questions to which participants were seeking answers, the framework within which they fit, and the directions that needed to be pursued.

Organizing around Issues

In the information society, the number of issues that transcend departmental barriers are increasing. Examples of this, including the environment (the Green Plan), competitiveness and the constitution, recurred in our discussions over the entire span of the project. A common denominator of those issues is that no one department has the mandate and resources to address them adequately, and the time horizon for their resolution extends beyond the usual time horizon of government decision-making.

A strong view was expressed that it is vital to find better ways of pulling together resources from across departments to address those issues. As one participant phrased it: "The question [this] raises is the ability of government to cope with the sorts of horizontal issues generated by the information society, . . . the need to develop a system that can adapt, and a type of decision-making that can deal with these sorts of problems." And another added: "If government can't deal with these sorts of real, complex cross-cutting issues, then it won't be much use to anybody in an information society."

One case study in particular examined the difficulties of addressing such issues, in an environment in which protection of departmental mandates and short-term crisis management are ever-present preoccupations. It examined an effort to place the issue of international competitiveness on the government's priority agenda, an effort that ultimately was at least partially successful (in what has come to be known as the "prosperity initiative"), but only after years of effort. What we heard described was governmental machinery that is increasingly incapable of coping with more interconnected issues in a more turbulent environment.

About the only way that system seemed able to address such issues was by a tremendous investment of time and effort by the most senior players, and as the number of such issues expands, that capacity at the top is being overloaded. In part as a result, there is more and more screening out of issues and ideas: ". . . if you are trying to work in an area of new ideas, the system isn't very friendly."

The problem, it was emphasized, was not incapacity or lack of goodwill on the part of the individuals involved. Indeed, the story was one of tremendous efforts to address a critical cross-cutting issue effectively. Rather, the case seemed to point to a growing mismatch between the capabilities of our political and administrative institutions and the demands generated by our social and technological environment. This is consistent with the recurrent finding in the research literature that changes in political and administrative institutions tend to lag behind basic changes in technology and the economy.

Discussion of the case study focused on the lessons that could be drawn on how to enhance the capacity of the government to deal with such issues, to deal more flexibly and more nimbly with cross-cutting problems. The challenge, as participants saw it, is to develop the capacity to organize ourselves more temporarily around issues rather than concentrating on longer-term organization around functions. One approach is to select a ministerial and/or senior official "champion" to marshall government resources around a particular issue for a defined time.

As one member of the roundtable stated: "That more temporary approach seems to me more attractive than trying to move a lot of bureaucrats around, which tends to be tremendously disruptive and reduces the overall effectiveness of the affected organizations for a long time." Besides, by the time the trauma of such reorganization is overcome, the issues requiring priority attention likely will have changed.

To organize effectively around issues, it was suggested, one of the first steps is to develop a common definition of the issue (a common interpretation or story):

> It is a question of learning what the challenge is, trying to define your challenge better and, in that context, to develop a different view of appropriate behaviour on the part of the government. . . . Once you can develop that common perception, then maybe process or even structural changes might be considered. But the fundamental first step is to create that new understanding, that new framework to guide our action.

The case study also illustrated the potential of such an approach. It found that:

> . . . people in other departments became excited about the need to think through these ideas, and the process gave them a framework. . . . The result of this whole exercise, perhaps one of its greatest benefits, is that within the government we developed a new kind of vocabulary. . . to use in thinking about this.

Once that broad framework is agreed upon, there can be wide scope for action at the working level to achieve it (and there also should be ways for the working level to participate in the definition of that framework). There is a need to explore and develop the ways in which this can be done more effectively. Amongst the steps that need to be explored are those that can strengthen the capacity for interdepartmental networking at the working level, and that can enhance the basis for more systematic consideration of proposals and their interrelation at the Cabinet level (what one participant called "the instruments of corporateness").

There also was a strong case made that this process of framing issues depended on a broader involvement of outside stakeholders:

> We can't operate on these sorts of issues in the old way and, in fact, not only do we need to involve other departments, but also players outside of government. The role we think we need to play on these sorts of horizontal issues is one of assembling resources that are needed both from around the government and from the private sector and the broader community, in order to address the question in a reasonable way. . . . What our effort has been about is to get a range of people within and outside of government engaged in a learning process that will help to understand and engage these issues.

At the broadest level, we saw that to organize more effectively and more flexibly around issues requires developing a learning process. What is needed is a learning process within government and with outside stakeholders, to frame the issue and establish a shared framework within which both governmental and non-governmental players can innovate better ways to deal with that issue. But such processes depend on government providing legitimacy to those issues and leadership to that process.

What is required to organize around issues often is most clearly exemplified in a crisis situation, and another of our case studies examined one such situation. The case told the story of how the Public Service organized to deal with the war in the Persian Gulf. We saw how bureaucratic hierarchy tends to be overwhelmed in those circumstances and is replaced by cross-functional and cross-departmental teams.

Those teams are organized to make sense of overwhelming amounts of information rapidly, anticipate the future and cut through bureaucratic hierarchy to get the job done. They operate as temporary learning systems, sharing information rapidly and widely, reaching conditional decisions based on incomplete information in a rapidly changing environment, examining alternative scenarios, acknowledging uncertainty and seeking continuously to improve their understanding and the effectiveness of their response.

One key to that process, we were told, is managing the interpretive framework being used to make sense of the situation by the various agencies and branches involved, and also seeking to ensure that a similar framework is adopted by outside interests who increasingly play an important role. The focus is not so much on management of information as on management of the frameworks within which information is interpreted (is translated into knowledge). Once those frameworks are established, the authority to get the job done in that context needs to be delegated as far down as possible, to facilitate rapid and flexible response.

Some Basic Principles of Organizing

Another case study enabled us to generalize this approach in terms of a basic principle of organizing in both the public and the private sectors. According to this view, managing and accountability is a matter of letting the people to whom you have given responsibility exercise it. The point is to identify priorities with them (a shared framework) and at the end of the year use a mixture of quantitative and qualitative measures to assess performance and update the framework (set future priorities).

This case study examined the effects of information technology on systems of accountability within the Public Service. One key design issue it raised was what the interval of accountability should be, or as it was phrased in the case study: "is a microsecond different than a year?" While the general view was that the appropriate interval would depend on the nature of the function, there was widespread support for the view that microsecond accountability was a contradiction in terms. As one participant put it:

> Generally speaking, if a superior has to be involved in the decision virtually in real time, then he or she must take responsibility for it. Otherwise, you should back away and let the people to whom you have given responsibility exercise it, and then come to your judgements, in some reasonable period, about how well they do.

There were a number of comments on the self-defeating nature of microsecond accountability (which information technology makes technically feasible). For example :

> Not only is there a question of artificial behaviour that people may be forced into, but it also has a horrendous effect on the time horizon of people. In the microsecond scenario you can't invest for the future, you are caught like the pension fund manager being measured on a constant basis so that you can never invest in anything that doesn't prove how brilliant you are in the next quarter. To empower people, you need to make them accountable for things, and just because you can control on an on-line basis, or monitor, doesn't mean that you should.

Others expressed the view that in most circumstances efforts at microsecond accountability would fail in any case because the "monitors" would be unable to handle the vast amounts of data that the accountability system would generate. In that view, those pressures would force the system back toward a more reasonable, periodic form of accountability:

> We are all human beings and we are going to use only a certain amount of information anyway, and the real challenge is how to design your information systems to reflect the reality and requirements of the management environment. The challenge is to develop information systems that will reinforce and support good and effective management.

Participants also saw important, untapped potential in information technologies that could be used to underpin not only better management but also more effective governance by providing measures of policy outcomes as well as program inputs. The idea is to provide an essential feedback loop that we can use to learn more effective ways to define and achieve policy objectives. As one roundtable member put it, we need to examine:

> . . . the positive potential being unleashed by the technologies, technologies that can provide much more informative and valuable measures of what our policies are accomplishing, and provide us with a new basis on which to make decisions and evaluate outcomes. We should be thinking more of the tremendous potential new technologies are providing us to develop more effective governance, rather than focusing on fine-tuning and automating older accountability systems.

Paul Strassman, a former senior executive of Xerox and a leading international authority on the organizational implications of information technology, reinforced these points, and underlined that simply automating existing bureaucratic arrangements actually can result in less effective operation. Instead, he emphasized, it is necessary to develop a client-focused organization, and use the technology to empower those in direct contact with the customer to mobilize the resources of the organization to provide service. For such an approach to be successful, those so empowered need to understand the framework and objectives within which they are operating, and the system needs to be structured in a way that fosters effective feedback and learning. He argued that:

> The industrial paradigm is hierarchical, it is procedure-driven and only the managers or staff people are supposed to think and everybody else executes, it is a command economy. In its last stage of development, an industrial-based society sucks more and more resources into overhead, and the result is declining productivity, increased debt and lower standards of living . . . due to an excessive accumulation of overhead.
>
> The information-based society [by contrast] is basically a society which concentrates on the utilization of human capital, of human knowledge, and does that by moving management down to the level where you can make decisions, and that frees up an awful lot of the overhead that has been absorbed in maintaining the top-down system of industrial-based society. The transition from an industrial-based society to a successful information-based society is one in which you can free an enormous amount of resources to do value-added work especially in the public sector.
>
> When you take an industrial, hierarchical structure and move it into a more complex environment how does it react? The paradigm is that you add another level, you add another consultant or another specialist so now instead of having 20 people to make a decision you need 80 people, instead of having decisions in six months you end up on a seven year product cycle (whereas the Japanese are on a three year product cycle) and you are dead. . . .
>
> Now what does an information-based society offer you? What it does basically is to say that your overhead costs are unviable, you cannot compete, people are getting declining amounts of services and they are unhappy. You must understand that if you accumulate more and more decision-making in a hierarchical structure you will have more and more unhappy people. So the information-based society leads you to question the basic structure and organizational processes, to look at the process itself. You need to look at the process and say is this an industrial-age process or is this a low cost, work integration, customer service process?
>
> Too many organizations are looking to information technology to bail them out and maintain the old industrial paradigm and the old hierarchy. There are too many people going around saying you can keep your existing organization as it is because the technology will save you and that is retrogressive and reactionary and basically won't work.

Strassman went on to discuss the sort of organizational approaches needed for an information society:

> . . . imagine a corporation where to increase productivity they have dismantled the hierarchical structure, moved to an organization built on problem-focused teams, so that when a problem arises people from different areas come together in a task-oriented team to fix it, and once the problem is solved the team disburses. People are housed in organizations and then they drop into specific configurations on a task basis and then go away. Extremely productive, no hierarchy, responsive, people have pride and accomplishment and so on. They also can be disbursed geographically, one member of the team can be in Toronto another in Ottawa and so on, linked by multimedia electronics.

> Now the problem potentially is that there is perfect memory in such a system of who has said what to whom. Now imagine an organization that is punitive, and you can imagine an expert system that will watch the error frequency of people participating in this organization and automaticallly generate pink slips. So I end up with a dossier on you which is a minute-by-minute profile of every goof you made. What will happen in those circumstances is that many people will withdraw and then what have you got?

> Now, on the other hand, take another kind of organization which says that errors are the way we learn. When you have too many errors perhaps we will give you another job. In other words you design jobs based on the premise that you want people to succeed and use the measurement of error frequency to implement that. Every human being in this world can succeed in some way, you just have to find the right level for each. So some organizational approaches can deal with the potential of the technologies far better than others.

Some Examples

In the course of the project, we encountered a number of concrete examples of how the technology can be used to empower staff and increase effectiveness. There also were some striking parallels in the sort of management model that seemed to work in each case. One of these examples was provided by Paul Strassman:

One of my favourite Canadian examples comes from BC Hydro. They have an enormous control centre in Burnaby from which they can remotely release water to generate electricity to the United States, trading it like pork bellies. So when they haggle you down a fraction of a penny they make the deal and the guy says well you can have it in 20 minutes, and then he goes and he looks at the weather forecast where is it going to rain, where the water is, and releases the water and it comes trickling down, generates the electricity which is then transmitted to Oregon. Behind all of that is a simulator which tells you what the opportunity cost of that kilowatt is in contrast with keeping it or selling it in the daytime to Alberta.

Now I think that is fantastic. There is no way you could make those sorts of decisions without that kind of background and we will be seeing more and more of that sort of thing and in fact will be equipping people fairly low down in an organization with such a capability. The idea of empowering people in governance is to give them the capability to make fairly complex judgements on services, and simulators now give us the capability today, at fairly low cost, to visualize the issues and make those judgements.

Another example was provided when we visited senior executives of Canada Post, and saw a demonstration of their new, information-centred management system. As Strassman had argued, Canada Post found it had to rethink it's structure and organizational process to take advantage of information technology and to operate more effectively in a turbulent environment. The turning point in their evolution came in 1985-86, when critical problems in the operation of Canada Post (highlighted in the Marchment Report) led to the creation of an internal task force to completely review and rethink the way in which the company operated. In that process, they reframed their understanding of the business they were in, realizing that:

... what we were really doing was selling time. You sell a time-sensitive product. You can buy an electronic product that has a commitment to it, you can buy priority courier, which at the present time is guaranteed delivery noon next day, you can buy the special letter mail, which is guaranteed delivery by 5:00 pm next day, or you can buy reliability on two days.

In order to deliver such a time-sensitive product: "Operations were completely restructured to be an assembly line from coast to coast and ultimately around the world." Also, the number of management levels were reduced from 11 to 6. Central to that restructuring was the institution of a sophisticated computerized information and communications system that permitted minute-by-minute tracking of organizational operations. Between 1985 and today, operational information has moved from requiring a minimum of six weeks to reach senior management to total instantaneity.

One of the most striking effects of that system is that it provides a common database and a highly visual presentation of the current state of operations that is accessible across the corporation in real time. It provides managers and employees at all levels with an up-to-date and shared view of the current state of operations and also permits the rapid updating and display of quantitative measures of performance so that any problems can be identified quickly and rapid, remedial action taken. It creates a shared information environment, and a common framework of a particular sort.

Canada Post appeared to exemplify some of the requirements for organizing in the information society, including a reduction in hierarchy, developing a common framework and database in the context of which decision-making could be delegated as close as possible to clients, making more effective use of human resources, and rethinking both products and processes in the context of the opportunities provided by information technology.

On the other hand, concern was expressed that the Canada Post system also exemplified some of the pathologies of microsecond accountability and wondered whether employees really were being empowered in that context. In this respect, Canada Post seemed to be a mixed example, both illustrating some of the potential benefits of adopting more information-based ways of organizing and, at the same time, still trying to preserve some of the industrial, assembly-line model of control.

A less dramatic example of the use of information technology to foster faster, more concise internal communications, more rapid decision-making, and a wider sharing of information, was provided by a case study that focused on the introduction of email in a government department. Although the email system introduced was rudimentary, discussion of the case, and of comparable efforts in which roundtable members had participated, highlighted a number of effects on the workings of the organization, and again reinforced some of the information-based organizing principles discussed earlier [the asterisks indicate the division between one speaker and the next]:

> Well, one thing I have noticed is that minutes have become a lot shorter and the format has tended to move more towards bullets rather than longer paragraphs. Actually, I think that makes for much more effective communication. . . . Also, the technology has very much increased the speed of communication and, so, shortened our turnaround time. But to do that we have had to change our internal management practices, and I think that underlines an important point, which is that success is not just the result of the technology, but very much depends on the way in which the organization uses it.

> ***

> One of the benefits of this system is that it allows for a more informal style of decision-making . . . a lot of matters that used to go through the hierarchy are now dealt with directly.

> ***

> One other benefit we have found in using these sorts of systems is that you can provide electronic authorization, and we are already starting to see some speeding up and eliminating of a lot of internal paper processes around issues like procurement. For example, our finance shop now will accept electronic authorization for travel.

> ***

> . . . the system is particularly valuable for providing service to clients. It facilitates communication, access to a common database, and eliminates telephone tag with a lot of people. . . .

The discussion also emphasized that:

> . . . it is a mistake simply to automate the existing bureaucracy, the management approach needs to be restructured and, most often, the technology is conducive to empowering employees at all levels. That's where the real benefits start to emerge.

The Limits of the Possible in the Public Sector

Throughout our discussions in the project, an important recurring question was the extent to which it is feasible to adopt information-based ways of organizing in the public sector. Clearly we can go a lot further than we have so far, but we still need to learn whether there are any necessary limits in what is possible owing to the differences between the public and private-sector environments. Some efforts have been made to allow parts of the public service to operate in a client-driven way, and these have sometimes run up against some of the constraints inherent in operating in a public-sector environment.

One of our case studies examined an effort to transform a branch of a department (the Bureau of Labour Information, which is responsible for providing information to the public on collective bargaining), into a client-centred, information marketing organization, though still operating within the apparatus of government. The organization streamlined its structure, reduced staff by a third and introduced a regime of cost recovery. It redefined its product line, eliminating some for which the market was insufficient, while restructuring others and adding new ones targeted at market segments. It undertook marketing intiatives to raise the profile of its information services, took steps to provide direct phone and computer access to clients, and changed the format of the information it disseminated to make it more useful and readable.

Initially these innovations resulted in a fourfold increase in client service, but very soon that increasing demand overwhelmed the organization's capacity to respond, and it was not possible to assign additional personnel to deal with the demand:

> ... we did a market research survey, which indicated that we could make a million dollars providing the information in a certain way, but what that study never considered was that to generate the product we would have to hire about 4,000 people, which, given PY constraints, wasn't going to happen. ... But that's another illustration of one way in which government bureaucracy is limited in its capacity to organize itself in a market-driven format.

To develop its capacity to respond to market demands, the organization urgently required high-level skills in the development of information technology systems, in the design and implementation of pricing and cost recovery regimes and in marketing. All of those skills were in very short supply within government, and government regulations, operating procedures and use of central services added further delay.

There also was limited capacity to contract for them outside. The marketing function, in particular, was seen as too central to the new mission of the organization to be contracted out. ". . . I guess the most basic issues we have run into have to do with the extent to which, in a government bureaucracy, we have the wrong people, with the wrong skill set, and so need a great deal of retraining and reorientation to make the new sort of approach feasible."

But the problems that the organization encountered were seen to be not just a lack of the right skills within the bureaucracy, but also a fundamental problem of culture:

> . . . once [the organization] reached a certain level of success (and this may be because of the bureaucratic culture), it thought it could stand pat. It did not realize that changing telecommunications technology and expectations require that any organization that is providing information, whether it is free or for cost, has continually to re-evaluate what it is doing, how it is doing it and the way it is delivering it, if it is to sustain success.

Conclusions

While many of those constraints no doubt can be remedied, we suspect others may be inherent in the public sector. At its most fundamental, the public sector operates on the principle of ministerial responsibility, which means that priority is always given to protecting and preserving the authority of the Minister. This can limit the extent to which a public-sector organization can be truly client-driven.

This may argue for the need to privatize or contract out as many functions as possible, leaving the public sector proper to focus on setting the framework for those functions, and on carrying out the irreducible set of functions for which Ministers must exercise direct responsibility. Such a model merits exploration. It is consistent with the general approach of information-based organizing, which stresses the establishment and management of the overall framework of interpretation and objectives and, in that context, enables a wide range of players to innovate and learn better ways to fulfill those objectives.

Harlan Cleveland expressed a comparable view at our inaugural roundtable:

> I grew up with the New Deal model that problems would be solved by the federal government—that once a problem was defined, a bureaucracy would be established with a building and with staff and it would deal with the problem. What I've come to realize is that while government does have a responsibility for fairness, it does not have to organize the carrying out of that responsibility as a government enterprise.
>
> We can use and should use the private and voluntary sectors. We can and should use an uncentralized approach. A decentralized approach is one where you keep the reins but get others to do the work. An uncentralized approach on the other hand, is 'a thousand points of light' and 'letting a thousand flowers bloom.' In this respect, I think Reagan sniffed it out right, because he expressed the view that government does not need to do everything.
>
> The mistake that Reagan made is to think that government should withdraw entirely, because that withdraws government from the fairness issues. You can only lead by withdrawal to a point. What we need to develop is a post-new deal approach. In this regard, I think it is a mistake to think Eastern Europe can and should simply adopt the current western capitalist model; rather we and they are both evolving toward something that hasn't been invented yet, toward a system that can provide growth with fairness.

In the Canadian context Ministers clearly have a responsibility for setting the policy framework within which public goods and services are provided. But it may be that in the information society it makes more sense to strengthen the capacity of the government to establish, monitor and give effect to that framework, its capacity to provide overall leadership, while leaving to special operating agencies, outside contractors or the workings of the marketplace the responsibility for the actual provision of services within that context. As one participant phrased it:

> In many cases, it may be best to envision a very small headquarters group serving a Minister setting the broad framework, while service delivery is provided through various kinds of agencies. That's a bit like the way things are organized in Sweden.

Participants concluded that this was one approach that merited further attention. While recognizing the political reality that in Canada in the past Ministers have tended to be preoccupied with "giving out money and cutting ribbons," participants generally concluded that:

> ... the system is changing, and the loss of legitimacy for government reflects that. People are becoming less and less comfortable with the notion of a politician coming out and giving them money, they increasingly expect more than that from government. Politicians who simply come out and provide money without being able to give a convincing case as to what they are trying to do in a broader sense are less and less credible as people become more sophisticated. So it may well be that there are developing some practical political reasons why we need a greater capacity to deal with conceptual issues, strategy, frameworks, vision, leadership and so on.

To the extent such an approach is pursued, there is a great deal of work to be done in defining what services can better be delivered by agencies or by the marketplace and which require continuing Ministerial oversight. There also is much work to be done in strengthening the framing capacity of government so that it can provide the context and leadership required for such an "uncentralized" approach.*

---

*The seeds of such approaches already have been sown, though often for different purposes. For example, over the years some useful preliminary work has been done in examining particular privatization and contracting out initiatives, and more recently in developing the new "special operating agencies." And there are valuable lessons (both positive and negative) to be drawn from earlier efforts to provide more effective support to Cabinet decision-making.

More basically, participants recognized that, in the information society, issues increasingly cut across departmental boundaries and require a time horizon that exceeds that of most government planning. We need to find ways, within a governmental structure premised on "vertical" departmental lines of accountability, to address this growing array of "horizontal" issues more effectively. Our earlier discussion of "organizing around issues" suggested a number of possibilities that we hope will receive further attention in that regard, and the next two chapters will examine several more. We need to learn how to deal with such cross-cutting issues not only in high-profile crisis situations, but also in normal day-to-day operations at all levels. We need to develop a culture and practice of working across departments on an issue-focused basis.

As the boundaries between public and private sectors dissolve in the information society, the process of framing issues depends increasingly on a broader involvement of outside stakeholders. The next chapter examines the process of consensus-building in the information society, and in that context explores other ways in which those shared frameworks, within and beyond government, can be created and renewed.

3

Forging Consensus in the Information Society

At the beginning of the project, the roundtable defined the issue of consensus-building in the information society in the following way:

> Similar to the trends in industry, government is experiencing both a process of globalization (as more and more issues are handled in supranational fora, networks and organizations) and a process of atomization, decentralization and democratization (as provinces, localities and various non-governmental groups become increasingly powerful players). These processes, taken together, vastly increase the number of relevant players that need to be incorporated into the process of governance in some fashion. Increasingly the issue becomes how is it possible to get everyone into the act and still get anything done?

> Government now finds itself, as never before, in a context characterized by mulitiple voices, as a wide range of groups in a more highly educated and informed society organize to assert a role in the governance process. Governance increasingly centres on the discovery of ways to harmonize and mobilize a wide diversity of interests to address public policy issues with which government alone cannot expect to cope. An increasing concern, in this context, becomes how to ensure that all relevant interests are brought forward and weighed, so that no one interest can capture the public agenda.

> At the same time, the very distinction between public and private sectors begins to blur as the growth of the service sector and the privatization and contracting out of government functions proceed, as new partnerships amongst the multiplying range of players in the governance process are made, and as new organizations are developed to demand a greater voice in that process.

This chapter outlines what the roundtable has learned in exploring the issue of consensus-building in an information society, and highlights the ideas and issues that we believe merit further attention. As in Chapter 2, these should not be read as final recommendations, but rather as a preliminary report on a learning process that we believe needs to be continued and to involve a wider range of participants.

The Importance of Shared Myths

We have found some striking parallels between the new ways of organizing outlined in the last chapter, and the ways of forging consensus that seem to be called for in the information society. In both cases the issue of establishing a shared framework is key. The need for such a shared framework at the societal level was underlined during our roundtable discussion with Donald Michael. At one point in the discusssion a paragraph from a *Foreign Affairs* article by William MacNeill was quoted:

> Myth lies at the basis of human society. That is because myths are general statements about the world and its parts, and in particular about nations and other in-groups, that are believed to be true and then acted upon whenever circumstances suggest or require common response. This is mankind's substitute for instinct. It is the unique and characteristic way of acting together. A people without a full quiver of relevant agreed upon statements, accepted in advance through education or less formalized acculturation, soon finds itself in deep trouble, for, in the absence of believable myths, coherent public action becomes very difficult to improvise and sustain.

In his presentation, Donald Michael situated this concern about shared myths at the centre of thinking about the implications of the information society for governance: "Democracy, as I understand it, is premised on a shared view of the world, of what is real and important, and when you have totally different worldviews (which is increasingly what we are seeing in the information society) then it's very difficult to forge consensus." According to Michael, the loss of boundaries generated by the information society, the multiplication of interests and the access that different interests have to the governance process, break down the shared world view on which legitimate collective action depends:

> To put it bluntly, the social construction of reality on which our government and governance process have been based, the stories we tell and that were told, that contained societies and gave order to them, are all dissolving. . . .

Michael argued that to deal with that breakdown of shared worldview, we need to develop the capacity continually to regenerate those shared frameworks, those shared stories, and to test them against rapidly changing environments. That means we need to develop a societal capacity to learn (and to learn how to learn) of a high order.

Societal Learning

According to Michael's thesis, societal capacity to learn depends on the development of a "new competence" on the part of governors, a new competence whose principal attributes include:

- acknowledging uncertainty;
- embracing error;
- moving from control to resilience as a metagoal of management and policy;
- developing the capacity to span boundaries; and
- becoming educators.

Such a societal learning approach also entails a quite different relationship between governors and governed:

> . . . if government is to model being learners, it seems to me one of the major implications of that is that you need to include in the learning process the people who are going to be the beneficiaries or the victims of the experiment. Instead of having the answers, experts would need to become resources to the participants, outlining what are the options and what are the consequences, so that the participants, the people, become part of the creation, part of the learning process. . . .

When challenged further on how realistic such an approach was, given the expectations of the public, the media and others, that governors will have the answers and will solve the problems, Donald Michael elaborated:

> ... what I am proposing is to engage people on a regular basis in trying to wrestle with these questions. When the government, by implication, says it will solve the problem it encourages the kind of attitudes and inappropriate demands you are talking about on the part of the public. I am arguing that we should discourage that and instead invite the public to join in what is, in effect, an R&D effort. . . .

At the same time, he was not optimistic about the possibility of integrating proliferating worldviews, through such learning processes, into a consensus in the short term: ". . . I think that in the circumstances that we are talking about, developing a single consensus is a very low probability. What's more realistic is management of multiple consensi with the hope that as the learning process develops, we may be able collectively to build some broader and more encompassing examples of consensus."

A complementary perspective was provided by Harlan Cleveland. In his view, consensus, and the shared framework of interpretation on which it is based, is not imposed, but rather emerges from a societal learning process, and the key role for government lies in facilitating and legitimating that process:

> There's a three-level model that I find useful in trying to think about this. At the first and broadest level are the people in general. At the middle level are leaders, the opinion leaders in society (in the U.S., there are about one million of those). And at the third level, are what I call policy announcers (what others refer to as policy makers). The leaders have the function of passing information back and forth, and in so doing let the consensus amongst the people develop. The bright political leader will then sniff out that consensus and announce it. Others may say that he had made policy. Really what he has done is to enunciate the consensus that had formed.

The Role of Leadership: Framing the Issues

A recurrent issue for participants in the project was the appropriate leadership role for government in such a societal learning process. Participants asked whether government did not have a responsibility to shape opinion, and also what constituted leadership in that context. One participant suggested that leaders have an intuition and can articulate something that rings true. Cleveland replied that:

> In fact, many people are involved in that process of shaping. For example, if I understand what some of you are saying, it may well be that one of the reasons that the Meech Lake constitutional agreement is a problem is because the people did not lead it. Your idea of government shaping opinion is very similar to the way people inside the beltway in Washington think.

> . . . it only rings true if the masses have decided, in a sense the leader is simply codifying that consensus. In this regard, history is unhelpful because we only have the history of the elite—we have very little information on where the general population stood. But informatization changes the interaction fundamentally, with many more people getting information about an issue and feeling that they can participate. That means that more than ever, the primary function of the elite is to codify that consensus as it forms.

At the same time, Harlan Cleveland argued that there were things that government could and should do to provide leadership and to foster the formation of consensus:

> One suggestion is that we have not been using information technology skilfully enough to this end. Would it not be possible to develop computer simulations that would enable a wide range of citizens and groups access to the essence of any public policy question? Traditionally, we have assumed that the general population can't understand the complexities of an issue, and have reinforced that by hiding behind our different specialist jargons. But what if every town had a facility which displayed simulations of issues and allowed members of the population to ask what-if questions, to explore the real implications and boundaries of policy issues? . . . The issue is to give the public the opportunity to manipulate the data, to ask what-if questions, and to learn.

If the key issues can be formulated in ways that citizens can understand, then a quick consensus can be developed. Since followers usually get there before leaders, the best way to accelerate the process of consensus building is to find a way for the followers to get there faster. The contrary situation is exemplified in the field of arms control which is totally dominated by an expert community, so that now the key constraint to getting new agreements is the great difficulty in bringing their elaborate constructs into line with a rapidly changing reality. It is a cautionary tale.

More broadly, Cleveland argued, government has a responsibility to frame issues in a fashion that people can understand and address:

This implies that we need to consult, for example on a budget, not by getting individuals to understand the technical detail in the way that public servants do, but rather to present the central dilemmas in their essence without too much technical refinement. I think you will find that a very large proportion of people have ideas on what can be done about issues like the deficit, and that by presenting issues in this way we will be facilitating the formation of exactly the sort of consensus we are searching for. So far, public servants are not very good at doing this, and that's one of the reasons why the focus on rethinking the process of consensus which has recurred in this conversation is so important.

Issues need to be encapsulated in a fashion that enables people to see the tradeoffs and implications and make a judgement. Often this requires leaders to fashion new metaphors that enable people to grasp the essence of the issues and of the choices that need to be made. Once a decision is made in this way on the broad issue (at the level of values), the technical details can be worked out by technical people. Overwhelming people with technical details is counter-productive.

These points were reinforced, and their relationship to the need to construct shared frameworks of interpretation elaborated, in a roundtable discussion of a case study on "public participation in decision-making in our system of government." (This roundtable occurred more than a year after the sessions with Donald Michael and with Harlan Cleveland.) The case study examined the changing roles of Parliament and the courts, and how citizens' rights and attitudes with respect to participation in governmental and judicial decision-making were changing. The discussion focused on lessons to be drawn from the experience of Meech Lake:

What you really need is a communicator who can take the set of more detailed proposals and encapsulate them into a few simple ideas which demonstrate that what we are talking about is whether we want to have a country or not. There is a need to encapsulate the ideas in a fashion that allows people to provide a judgement, on the basis of which others then can deal with the details.

* * *

So then you ask yourself, why are we going to such lengths to get all of these other detailed proposals out in public?

* * *

That's a very good question. I think a real issue with the new set of proposals is that they haven't been encapsulated in a way that the public can deal with, so the public is milling around trying to deal with things they really can't deal with. . . .

* * *

Maybe the role of government, then, is to try and present the issues that people can deal with, rather than giving them long lists of detailed stuff that are essentially grist for the bureaucrats' or technocrats' mills.

Encapsulating issues in that way, some participants emphasized, is not simply a matter of getting out the facts: it always involves selecting and interpreting information, it involves helping people to translate data and information into knowledge they can use. As Donald Michael had emphasized, people make sense of information in terms of their own frameworks of interpretation, in terms of shared myths, metaphors and stories. In the discussion of the same case study, participants explored these points:

Does that raise the question of the degree to which communication, especially in an information society, is all about—metaphors and images? The essential debate about the Thomas/Hills confrontation was done in a language of metaphors, images, and we see the same thing unfolding with respect to the distinct society. What does it mean? It means nothing, but it means a lot. In the context, it becomes charged with meaning.

When you are talking about communication and information you are not talking about a series of words. It is the context, the overall pattern that is important and provides meaning. . . . So communication in an information society is not a matter of data or particular words, it's a matter of communicating images and metaphors and building a shared context. It would suggest that the solution to things like the constitutional debate is not so much to change the answers or to provide more detailed data, as it is to change the questions, to change the metaphors.

* * *

I think that's what I have been struggling for, the problem isn't the answers, it's the questions.

* * *

... That's a very good point, because if you don't tell a story that makes sense of all of this information, someone else is going to come up with a story that will make sense of it in a different way. That is maybe what's happening with the government's constitutional proposals. Other people are spinning stories to make sense of the 28 points, and so far the government has not been very effective at spinning a story that can provide people with an understandable overall image of what they are trying to accomplish.

Participants suggested that such a capacity to frame issues in a form that could generate understanding and consent, such a capacity to create and renew shared frameworks of interpretation, was a key function of leadership in the information society:

Much of what we are talking about comes down to political leadership. The human mind is not constructed to be able to cope with masses of facts and masses of argument. It has to reduce things to some sort of simple shorthand, into themes and images. I think most citizens have a fairly good sense of their own interests and of where they want to be. The role of political leaders is to translate issues into some kind of terminology that people can relate to.

Consensus-building: some Lessons from Experience

At another roundtable we discussed in some detail a number of concrete examples, both from Canada and from other jurisdictions, where efforts at consensus-building had been undertaken. Arthur Kroeger, Deputy Minister of Employment and Immigration, drew lessons from his experiences in a number of such efforts, both successes and failures (the joint Government-Indian process, the Crow rate, National Economic Summit, Labour Force Strategy). He drew on that experience to define a pragmatic approach to marshalling a consensus of interests to achieve concerted action.

His conclusion was that the most successful processes were ones in which the government's role was to provide a framework (define the context, the objectives, the process), involve interests, make sure they understand their stakes, let negotiation occur without interference, and "announce" the results. As he summarized his view:

> The first point is that there has to be a recognition on the part of the players that there is a problem. For example, the wheat pools didn't want to pay more to move their grain, but they knew that there was a problem, the grain transportation system was getting more and more rickety, some of the mountain main lines were at risk and so they just couldn't turn their backs . . . That is the first requirement.

> The second requirement is, if at all possible, avoid dealing with single interest groups one at a time. My experience suggests that if you can put them in a situation where they, and not the government, have to make the trade-offs, you have a much better chance of achieving a consensus. That's far more effective than if government receives a bunch of briefs and tries to make the trade-offs itself. . . .

> The third point, and perhaps the most important of all, is that the players have to see that their self-interest is in play [in reaching a compromise]. They have got to realize that there are risks in perpetuating the status quo [and] risks in simply rising up in total opposition. . . . A lot of single-interest groups can be persuaded at the end of the day that they better do something bad in order to prevent something worse. . . .

> Just a couple of other quick observations. While I didn't realize this at first, I am coming to the view that it is better if government can establish an explicit framework of what is and what isn't negotiable and then not even be in the room. That is what we did both in the case of the Crow and in the case of the Labour Force Strategy. If you are in the room, the interests have to play to you, they are all grand-standing trying to influence you, but if you are not even there they have got to be more serious in dealing with each other. . . .

A second important observation is that it's best to do it all out in the open, with no hidden agendas. Information leaks, but if everything is out in the open that doesn't make a difference. Finally, take lots of time, be prepared to take lots of time. The Crow took us three and a half years. The exercise with the private sector on the labour market already has been going for nearly two years and it will be at least another year before we know whether our training board is going to work. You have got to allow the thing to percolate, you have to allow enough time for everybody to understand it and to be comfortable with it, to make sense of the information, if it is going to work.

When challenged on whether such an approach (setting the framework and letting the players reach a consensus in that context) constituted an abdication of government leadership, Kroeger replied:

> ... in some areas where we do exercise leadership we do so by establishing a process within which stakeholders can decide. However we define the framework and even the time frame. Fundamental to making that kind of process work is the prospect that if the stakeholders do not manage to reach an agreement, government will take whatever action it sees fit. ...

At the same roundtable Steven Waldhorn, the Director of the Center for Economic Competitiveness of SRI International described for us the experience of SRI in seeking to develop consensus on regional economic strategies in jurisdictions around the world. The particular examples he used included projects in India, the midwest U.S.A., Spain, Baltimore, Eastern Germany and Hong Kong.

His conclusions largely mirrored those of Arthur Kroeger, but added an emphasis on the value of providing a common information base, in particular solid analysis in regional contexts where interests are clearly understood. He also emphasized the value of a process which involves an even larger role for non-governmental players, including the media. He talked about the importance of combining analysis and process:

> ... generally we are invited in by someone with a personal vision, a champion. Could be a politician, or more likely a businessmen, and while there are incredible differences among the types of champions, there are basic similarities in the kind of role they play and in their commitment to the betterment of their region. .... Then we begin to slowly build a

leadership group and begin the process of analysis that will lead to a report or several reports on what steps could be taken to enhance the competitiveness of the region.

. . . Once the analytical reports are done, then it's a question of getting different stakeholders in a group around a table like this, and what follows is a socialization process that takes six or nine months. Typically the end product is some kind of adjusted understanding and then all of the players go off with this new understanding and work it through the regular processes of decision-making, legislation and so on.

Waldhorn emphasized the tremendous leverage that such a shared vision (what Donald Michael and others had referred to as shared myths and stories, a shared framework of interpretation) can provide:

A vision might sound like something mystic but in fact what it does is give people a logic to help them to understand themselves in a different way. In the case of Nebraska it was understanding that we are not a corn growing state, but the place you reach in the U.S. when somebody dials an 800 number, we are an information processing state. When you give people a new vision, then you are able to develop an alternate rationale for their institutions whether they be scientific or business or educational. It is this blending of analysis with process to generate a new vision, that can be so important in moving towards consensus.

In the discussion, members of the roundtable tried to draw some generalizations from the presentations that had been made by Arthur Kroeger and Steven Waldhorn about what was needed to generate a shared framework to provide the basis for a workable consensus. One element that was underlined was the importance of developing a consensus on the definition of the problem:

I feel in listening to our discussion that in all of the cases of processes that worked, an important factor was that we understood, that there was a consensus on, what the problem was that we were trying to solve. I think part of the Canadian dilemma at the moment is that we do not know yet what we are trying to resolve with respect to the national debate. Because we don't have a sense of the definition of the problem we are dealing with, we are not getting a solution or the parameters within which we can seek solutions.

Another point emphasized was the need for a common database. In that context it was underlined that there was no objective data and that the issue always was how to make sense of data, how to interpret it (how to translate data into knowledge). The suggestion also was made (echoing an earlier comment by Harlan Cleveland) that information and communications technology could help in that process of building a shared interpretive framework:

> I . . . wonder whether there is not in fact a tool now available to us that can have a dramatic potential effect on our ability to forge consensus? I am thinking, for example, of the experiment in Oregon, using the capacities of computers and spreadsheets to circulate compilations of potential costs and benefits of major policy issues to a wide range of the population, so that people could manipulate the spreadsheets, make their choices and imagine the consequences.

> One benefit is that it makes trade-offs far more visible, so that interest groups would recognize that everything is not possible. But, secondly, such a process may enable legislators to pass legislation and to take public policy actions out of greater public understanding of the nature of the world and the implications of the choices to be made. . . .

Another case study, which dealt with the question of business governance in an information society (focusing on lessons learned in attempts to modernize Canada's legislative framework in the areas of competition policy and intellectual property), also underlined that an important element in creating a framework within which a consensus may emerge is to work on common information, common definitions, so we don't spend our time arguing about the data but instead talk about issues and solutions. Like Arthur Kroeger, the case study emphasized that it is preferable to develop multi-stakeholder processes of co-operative policy development where government can be in a position to play an honest broker role (again managing the framework and the process).

An important question raised about such an approach was the degree to which a consensus brokered amongst special interests would represent a position that was in the public interest:

> What concerns me about that is the notion that by accommodating a whole range of interest groups you somehow end up with the right policy. I don't believe that. I think at the end of the day it's important for Parliament to make

a determination, after consultation to be sure, but the result needs to be more than simply summing up the various interests represented at the table.

***

I agree, I think this concept of multi-stakeholder determination is moving us much closer to the U.S. system and the role Congress has played in turning policy-making into a log-rolling exercise. The result, and that's a danger I hope we will find a way of avoiding here, is that policy-making ends up being essentially a question of brokering amongst the stakeholders, so policy becomes an issue of managing that process as opposed to actually determining what is in the public interest.

***

But I don't think the other extreme of developing policy in isolation and imposing it on the private sector is any better. . . . I am certainly not advocating completely expropriating the government's involvement in policy development; but, even if it does not result in consensus, an effective consultation process seems to me to be essential. It gives the government the benefit of hearing the viewpoints of conflicting interests, and challenging its own perceptions and plans against those viewpoints. I think that sort of consultation process, and the enrichment of the information base for policy development that it provides, has resulted in the development of better, more balanced policy.

Generally, roundtable members concluded that there was a need to develop more consensus-based approaches to governance. To do so would require a change in the public service culture, from one of confrontation to one of consultation and mutual learning. As one participant phrased it:

How do you get people, who are used to notching their belts with convictions, to think about getting compliance in other ways? I think that is a general problem that the government faces. Especially with the diminishing resource base, it is going to become more important to lever resources to get compliance using alternative methods.

The Limits of Regulation in the Information Society: the Case of Telecommunications

The need for such alternative methods was driven by the recognition that more traditional approaches are less and less effective in dealing with the realities of governing in an information society. For example, regulatory processes that rely on a quasi-judicial procedure, a complex apparatus of documentation and hearings, and costly, time-consuming litigation often are too cumbersome for the information economy.* This was exemplified in two case studies that focused on the telecommunications sector. The presenter of one case study outlined the growing difficulties encountered in trying to apply the traditional regulatory approach to the telecommunications sector:

> ... the development of these networks is running beyond the capacity of political institutions to control, both at the national and at the international level. ... The old means of subsidies and regulations and so forth are not really an option in a borderless, highly competitive world. There really are not now, nor will there be in any foreseeable future, effective international regulatory mechanisms. Those that do exist focus essentially on standard setting, allocation of the spectrum and so on.

> And, in any case, the reality of globalization means that one of the reasons for regulation in the past; namely, the existence of national monopolies, increasingly no longer is the case. What you are dealing with more and more looks like a competitive marketplace, and so we need to ask the extent to which special regimes still are needed to regulate that marketplace. ...

> ... one area that's open to serious question (about the ability and desirability of regulation) is the question of national ownership. That issue has been a staple of telecommunications policy around the world, in fact

---

* Throughout the project concern was expressed about the appropriateness and costs of litigation-based approaches in the information society. In addition to the concern about regulatory processes elaborated here, other discussions (particularly the discussion of the case study on 'participation in decision-making in our system of government') questioned whether the adversarial court system is the best place to deal with the balancing of policy issues that the Charter often raises. It also questioned whether the courts have the information and understanding of an issue necessary to make those kinds of determinations. Participants felt there was a need to explore better (more accessible, less costly and cumbersome) ways in which citizens might establish and defend their rights and resolve disputes.

in most places the government owned the carrier: telecom services were provided by the Post Office. In that respect the situation in Canada and the U.S.A., where private enterprises were significantly involved, was rather unusual until recently. Now the question is being raised that if networks are the key infrastructure of the information society, is it more important to have state-of-the-art networks, even if they are owned by AT&T rather than by Telecom Canada, or is it more important to maintain Canadian ownership and control?

Another question is whether we need to keep cable and telephone separate? Why are we still pretending they are two different businesses? Why should we prevent telephone companies from delivering a video signal to your home? . . . As a matter of regulatory policy we try to keep these two industries separate, while market forces and technological developments are pushing them to integrate.

. . . on the issue of content, it's often said that the networks of the future will allow us to choose from hundreds of programming sources, instead of going down to the video store to rent a video. We don't require Canadian content regulations in video stores, and, as people shift from going to video stores to rent the tapes to actually calling for them on-line through the network, is it really rational (and is it even feasible) to continue to require Canadian content rules?

. . . the reality is that our ability to control is largely being eliminated [in any case] by the way in which the technology is evolving. Take, for example, the so-called 'Death Stars,' direct to home satellite broadcasts which are projected by the Americans to be able to supply upwards of 100 channels. Those broadcasts will be able to be picked up by small dishes not much larger than a pizza, that will be very affordable for everyone. And, of course, fibre optics is another technology by which a very wide range of programming and information services will be available in all of our homes. The ability to regulate that on a national basis is very, very limited.

One response suggested to these difficulties was to shift the locus of the regulatory process from the national to the international level, to cope with an increasingly globalized marketplace:

I think we are approaching a very important conclusion, which is that one of the products of this techno-economic-social revolution that is taking place and that we call the information age, is a profound piece of international harmonization and it is irresistible. In the interconnected information society almost all efforts at domestic law regulation are counter productive. We need to make our decisions in an international context recognizing those global realities.

For example, it seems to me that if Germany was our neighbour and not the United States, we wouldn't have a federal budget deficit. Many of our current problems have to do with the degree to which we already have developed our policies in a North American context. What this means to me is that we have a very strong vested interest in lobbying for international regulatory structures and distributional structures. It is in the Canadian interest to do whatever we can to promote effective international regulation in the public interest in all of those areas where domestic regulation no longer makes sense.

Others pointed out that in some areas no sort of regulation, domestic or international, was feasible, while in other cases domestic regulation probably still made sense:

> ... We have to recognize that in the information society some things simply are not regulable, and that when you get into areas like telecom, broadcasting, fibre optics, and so on the very notion of harmonization of regulation at any level is futile. The regulatory approach preserves the notion that somehow you can control and order things. But what we increasingly need to recognize in the information age is that there are some areas of activity where that simply is not possible, you just have to let her rip and no one can stop it.

> ***

> But I think we need to be very careful about over-generalizing here. The case study illustrates a number of areas where it's very questionable that regulation is appropriate or even feasible. It shows a number of areas where, in fact, it has had a counter-productive effect. But, I think, we need to look more closely on a case-by-case basis to see where there is anything that potentially can and should be regulated in the public interest, where the better options are to look at some international form of regulation, and where we need simply to say that this is not an area where regulation is appropriate at any level. There is an enormous amount of analysis to be done.

Consensus-based Alternatives to Regulation

While recognizing that there were cases in which domestic regulation still made sense, participants generally expressed the view that in the information society those cases were becoming less and less prevalent, and that there was an urgent need to explore new approaches. As one member of the roundtable phrased it:

> The point that the case is trying to underline is that there are a spectrum of approaches we can take, and that while sometimes it's necessary to have regulations operating at its most ponderous, at the moment it seems to me that we are applying those legal regulatory approaches far too indiscriminately and without regard to its downside.

> . . . The Japanese contrast is interesting. At the end of the Second World War they were endowed with a whole range of regulatory institutions on the U.S. model, but over a period of five or six years those institutions all were rejected. They had a very different attitude towards the way in which the public interest can be included in decision-making, one that came out of their very different culture. Their approach, which is based on the development of consensus in a relatively homogeneous society, seems to be working very well relative to the more adversarial and litigious approaches that we have tended to adopt.

The roundtable explored some possible Canadian versions of such consensus-based approaches, alternative ways in which the public interest might be safeguarded. One possibility discussed was that of stakeholder summits:

> One question I was wondering about is whether the recent summit in Montreal on broadcasting might offer an alternative to the regulatory approach, one that has some parallels to the Japanese case? As I understand it, the Minister had in Montreal all of the big broadcasters and cable companies and the various producers of value-added services and, basically, after a discussion of the problems that they all faced, the Minister told them to come back to him with a consensus view within six months on what needed to be done. In some respects that reminds me of what Arthur Kroeger told us a few months ago about the consensus-development procedures used in the case of the Crow rate. Is there the beginnings of an alternative approach there?

***

Well perhaps, but the problem with that particular example is that I think what we are really seeing is an industry that has made some wrong investments now banking on the government to protect them. The Minister is asking what should I do to protect you and asking them to work out an approach, but a more sensible approach in this case would be to recognize that things like direct broadcast satellites are going to happen and there really is no question of stopping it in any effective way. We should have learned that from our earlier unsuccessful attempts to stop satellite dishes, or the British efforts to deal with off-shore radio stations. . . .

***

But I think the process does point to a useful alternative approach to dealing with these sorts of issues. And the range of interests who were represented around the table provide some protection against the sort of danger you are talking about.

***

Well, I wonder. I think that what we are likely to get out of that process is a consensus that will represent a trade-off amongst those special interests, that is almost certain not to be equivalent to the public interest.

***

So in a sense what you are saying is that the missing player at the meeting in Montreal was the spokesman for the public interest?

***

Yes that's it exactly. . . . For the kind of alternative approach you are talking about to work effectively it's essential to make efforts in advance to be sure that people who don't have a direct interest in that issue, or aren't aware of it, are involved in some fashion. It is important to take an active role to ensure that the interests of those who are not part of a well-organized group are effectively represented in some fashion. The government needs to design the consultative process so that there is some reasonable hope that whatever consensus emerges from around that table there is some resemblance to the public interest.

Another possibility explored was "faster regulation" (which seemed in essence to be a way of increasing the "requisite variety" of the regulating system):

While we are waiting to solve all of these deeper problems, though, I wonder if there may be some real benefits to be gained by looking at ways of speeding up the machine. For example, we all know about the differences between the

American and the Japanese auto industries in terms of how long it takes to design and produce a new model. In the American companies, in order to match the Japanese, they have started to incorporate a number of social and technological changes designed to speed up their own process.

One of the interesting by-products of those changes has been a real shift in culture away from the confrontational union versus management approach (which in some ways seems to me to be quite analogous to the regulatory process we have been talking about) towards a more co-operative culture. I guess what I was wondering is whether there is not a benefit to be gained in finding ways to speed up the machine involved in regulation and perhaps in so doing, in some small way, to begin to transform the culture of that system?

Other ideas canvassed included the use of Alternative Dispute Resolution techniques and the development of information-based ways of enforcement (for example, using positive and negative publicity to encourage compliance).

A number of suggestions were made on the need to find ways to use market mechanisms more effectively to encourage compliance (the trading system in pollution permits was one example cited). Such market mechanisms can be seen as special cases of the learning approaches that seem better able to cope with the turbulent and interconnected world of the information society. But for such market-based approaches to work, some participants argued, required a greater emphasis on framework issues of distribution and social contract:

... it seems to me that one of the most important implications of what we all have been saying around this table with respect to the information revolution is its distributional consequences. One of the real reasons that markets fail is because of a maldistribution of resources and income. The market can't work very efficiently if you don't have a sufficient number of players with the means to enter into transactions in the marketplace. It would seem to me that one of the implications of the argument that we should allow market forces to work, is that in order for that to happen we need to do something about accessibility problems by ensuring that there is enough distribution of income so that there will not be pressure on governments to intervene in the marketplace in other ways to restore the balance. . . .

***

Yes, I agree, and there are some leaders in the business community who are beginning to see that, although it's not anywhere near the predominant view yet. But some are beginning to argue that we need to pay attention to the basic social contract which is the essential underpinning if markets are to work effectively.

There seems to be a blind spot about this in English-speaking countries with a Lockean liberal heritage, and this is exacerbated by these technologies which can lead to further atomization. Instead it makes a lot of sense, and in fact it may be essential, for English-speaking societies to learn from the more organic societies in Japan or Continental Europe, who seem to have found a more effective mixture of social contract and effective markets. Canada, with its Red Tory tradition, should have an advantage over the United States in this regard, although it's far from clear that we are moving in that direction at this point.

Conclusions

Many of these views were summed up near the end of the project in a roundtable discussion of a case study on the changing nature of public consultation in the information society:

Earlier on someone referred to the notion of information as power and for a long time in my experience in government that was a fundamental belief, and making information scarce was important power. But I guess I am with Don Michael in thinking that as we move into the information age, the dissemination of information is the source of real power, and trying to keep it secret and husband it is to invite the sort of loss of legitimacy and fragmentation that we have been discussing. The government that is going to govern more wisely is the one that has more skill in disseminating information and in assisting in the learning process of transforming data and information into knowledge. . . .

When we speak about consultation I think we still too often deal with it in an old fashioned way, as legitimating essentially what has been happening in any case, instead of understanding its potential to develop the collective degree of understanding that enables any collective action at all. For all of the reasons we have been talking about, one of the real dilemmas we face in the information society is how to establish sufficient collective understanding and collective will to enable any public action to be undertaken effectively and legitimately. . . .

***

. . . I think that's generally right. The challenge is to form a common understanding, a common framework, and in that context issues can be resolved. I remember once talking to the Chief Operating Officer of a Fortune 500 company. . . about human resource development at a conference on that issue. He said to me that if the Japanese were at that meeting they wouldn't understand a word that people were saying because they just don't think in those terms. To them the issue wasn't human resource development, it wasn't training, that's not what they talk about. The issue for them is one of social contract.

Once you have that fundamental framework, that fundamental contract, established, then all the rest flows from that. But if you don't have that framework, all of the tactics and techniques are not going to help you very much. It seems to me all of the discussion we have been having about techniques of consultation is really a symptom of our problem rather than a solution. The issue is to find ways to construct and renew that common framework, that social contract. . . .

A recurring theme throughout the roundtable's discussions of consensus-building in an information society was the critical importance of generating such a shared framework, shared myths, stories and interpretations, in the context of which a consensus can be generated. This bears a striking parallel to the model of information-based organizing discussed in the last chapter, which involves the development of a shared vision and framework of objectives in the context of which a wide range of players can be given wide lattitude to innovate and learn better ways to meet those objectives.

The roundtable explored a variety of ways in which such a shared framework might be built. A common denominator of those approaches was the need to develop a process of societal learning to cope with the turbulence of the information society. One element of doing that would be for governors to adopt a new ethic, what Donald Michael referred to as "the new competence" (embracing error, acknowledging uncertainty, moving from control to resilience and so on), and a new relationship of governors and governed. Another was to make use of information technology to enable citizens to grasp the essence of a policy issue and the implications of the various choices available (what some referred to as a shared spreadsheet). The roundtable discussions emphasized the leadership role that governments needed to play in that context, in particular in framing issues in terms that people could understand, and in structuring the process so that the balance of perspectives represented were more likely to result in a consensus that would be in the public interest.

There also was growing skepticism expressed about the extent to which it was possible and desirable to control the information society using traditional legal and regulatory mechanisms. Experience in other jurisdictions, such as Germany and especially Japan, suggest that consensus-based mechanisms may be more effective ways to safeguard the public interest in the information society. The roundtable explored a number of these, including the use of stakeholder summits, market-based approaches, faster regulation, alternative enforcement (including alternative dispute resolution and information-based enforcement mechanisms).

There was a strong sense that such approaches needed to be explored in more detail in the Canadian context. In the end, at the global level as well as the domestic, those alternative, consensus and learning-based approaches may be the most viable ways of governing in an information society.

4

Strategic Use of Information

An important theme in the project has been how to make better use of information, both how to make sense of incoming information from a wide range of sources, and how best to communicate with the general public and stakeholders. At the outset of the project, the issue was described in the following way:

> In both the public and private sectors (in the face of huge volumes of data and much richer communications links) the most important skill increasingly is the strategic use of information: developing the conceptual and other mechanisms needed to translate data into information, and information into knowledge, and ensuring that the most pertinent information is provided to the relevant people to make a given decision. A range of information translation and related intermediary functions are growing up in the public and private sectors to help to meet this increasing demand.

Developing these better ways of using information, these more effective ways of translating a wide range of data into useful information and knowledge, is basic both to the information-based ways of organizing discussed in Chapter 2, and to the ways of forging consensus in an information society discussed in Chapter 3. Central to both is the need to develop a common context, a shared framework of interpretation. This chapter outlines what we have learned in exploring these questions and highlights the ideas and issues that we believe merit further attention. As in previous chapters, these should not be read as final recommendations, but rather as a preliminary report on the issues and on some promising ways of addressing them.

Governing and the Construction of Knowledge

At our inaugural roundtable, Harlan Cleveland had emphasized the distinction between data, information and knowledge. Data are raw facts, information are those facts refined and organized into some pattern, but a pattern not yet internalized ("the newspapers we have not read"). Knowledge is information that we have internalized and which is made meaningful by being situated within the context of our own frameworks of interpretation. As the project proceeded, we came to see the construction of knowledge more and more as central to the process of governing in an information society. As one group of participants phrased it toward the end of the project:

> ... when we talk about the problems of governing in an information society what we are fundamentally addressing is the fact that we have not found a way, within government, to take information and translate it and develop it, either for our own internal purposes or for purposes of dealing with external constituencies. What it comes down to is that we need more people, and I guess they are knowledge workers, people who can take a whole bunch of information, share it within the system and outside the system, and turn it into something that becomes digestible and useful by ourselves as bureaucrats and by Canadians. .... And as long as we keep talking about information and the information society, we are talking about the wrong thing. We should be talking about governing in a knowledge society or in a learning society.

The ways in which the construction of knowledge is central to the governing process was brought home to us most clearly in a case study of "the relationship of science and technology information to government decision-making." That case demonstrated that what was key for governance was not basic scientific data or information, but rather the very different ways in which that information was understood (was translated into knowledge) by politicians, officials, scientists, the media, interest groups and so on.

As the amount of scientific information has proliferated, a thriving industry in making sense of that information, in repackaging it for particular purposes, has emerged. It is those secondary repackagers who have the strongest influence on the policy process.

Increasingly, participants concluded that understanding and better managing that interpretive process was fundamental to effective governance:

> It seems to me one of the interesting things this case illustrates is both the positive and the negative aspects of the interpretive, intermediary function of packaging information and inserting it into the policy process. On the positive side, the packaging process can encapsulate issues and clarify what the questions are that need to be addressed. I remember a senior official in the mid-eighties doing a very good job of that in the area of energy policy where he demonstrated that the real issue was not self-sufficiency nor price control, but really economic development and the environment. Those were the areas where the decisions are important at the margin, where you could have the most leverage.

> The downside is illustrated by the recent concern about meningitis in Ottawa, or the alar scare for apples in Washington state. In those cases the way the media or interest groups packaged the information stampeded the decision-making process into making bad or unwarranted decisions. So the packaging process can work for both good and ill, which, I guess, underlines the importance of understanding it and better managing it.

> ***

> I don't think that the senior official in the mid-eighties actually got it right when he converted the energy issue from a self-sufficiency question to an environment and regional development question. . . . amongst other things that has resulted in some very, very bad and expensive regional development decisions, including Husky and Hibernia and that sort of stuff.

> It would be better to frame the energy issue in terms of Canadian expertise in an area of exportable technologies, an area where we can attack world markets and try to increase Canada's wealth. For example . . . a Canadian firefighting company put out three times as many oil well fires in Kuwait as any other company. So maybe it would be better to frame these kinds of issues in terms of what we need to make Canada more competitive globally.

> ***

> It's interesting to see what the different interpretations have been of the nature of the issues in this [energy] policy area. We've moved from issues of price and self-sufficiency, to issues of environment and regional development, and now we're talking about it in terms of the competitiveness agenda. We're re-interpreting it again in terms of today's issues, today's frame. . . .

We've heard in this case study that scientists tend to frame issues in one way, and politicians frame them in another way, and the media frame them in yet another way, and special interest groups frame them again in another way. It seems to me that one of the essential questions for us is what role is government going to play in this interpretive, framing process?

As the roundtable explored these questions further, it underlined the role of government in helping to translate across different perspectives, in helping to foster the creation of shared interpretations, shared knowledge:

> ... the science and technology case underlines how different communities of interpretation exist, whether it is scientists or politicians or bureaucrats or journalists or whatever. It seems to me that's a reality that goes well beyond the area of science. And I guess that's another way to think about the basic question that we discussed earlier of what is the role and capacity of government to create some sort of dialogue amongst those different communities with their different ways of interpreting and their different languages. What are the ways of reaching some sort of understanding, some sort of consensus, given the different world views they exhibit?

> ***

> It seems to me one of the implications of that is that government needs to pay more attention to that process of packaging and disseminating information to the various communities. ... Governments need to train or hire or somehow find people with the skills to handle information and to handle the process of translating across those different communities of interpretation.

But participants also were clear that this was not a task that government alone could accomplish. There also was a need to increase the extent to which some players from all sectors of society were prepared to play a role in that process of translation, in the construction of shared knowledge, of a shared community of interpretation:

> I think we see in all professions a process whereby a group of those professionals become 'public policy specialists,' they become intermediators and the moment they take that decision they begin to grow away from their professsion. The pure practitioners of the profession tend to disesteem those intermediators and, in that respect, I don't think the science culture is much different than, say, social scientists or lawyers or

whomever. But probably science has not come as far yet in establishing that cadre of public policy specialists.

One of the realities of the information society, it seems to me, is the growing realization of the fundamentally important roles played by those intermediators. They provide the means for communicating between the various specialities and for focusing them towards a range of public issues that necessarily require the bringing together of multiple skills and multiple perspectives.

It seems to me we need to foster a cultural change in which a greater value is placed on the role of intermediating, of diffusing and translating information, of translating a wide range of information into knowledge that's useful for broad decision-making. As that culture change occurs it seems to me that the role of public policy specialist will become more acceptable to those in the scientific community.... In a sense we need to foster a process where scientists [for example] are willing to take on more of a statesman role.

A key challenge for governance in an information society, as another participant summed up the discussion, is the "need to create a common language, a community of discourse amongst those coming from very different perspectives, with very different specialist languages and interests. How do you create a common framework within which communication can occur and differences can be reconciled?" The creation of such a shared framework and language is an essential part both of coordinating action within the government, and of building consensus more broadly within society.

Constructing a Shared Framework within Government

Scenarios

Scenario planning is one powerful tool for constructing a shared framework of interpretation within an organization, or across organizations, that was recommended to us separately by Donald Michael, Harlan Cleveland and Paul Strassman. The scenario approach has been developed and applied most extensively within Royal Dutch Shell, and to explore that technique in more detail we met with Arden Brummell, formerly a member of the scenario group at Shell headquarters in London, and currently an executive with Shell Canada.

As Brummell described it, Shell uses scenarios to develop a shared mental map amongst the managers in its highly decentralized operations. Scenarios, as Shell conceives them, are a means to an end: a way of setting an external context within which people can begin to develop options and strategies for their specific operations. They are intended to provide alternate visions of what the future business environment and larger societal context may be like. They are used to generate a set of possible different future contexts and to provide a basis for looking at an organization's own capabilities to respond.

They provide a shared framework within which people can examine particular decisions. "You select that framework, that scenario, and analyze the given problem within that context. Scenarios are seeking different logics, on the basis of which you can spin out a story about how the future will unfold." It is that process of creating and renewing shared frames that Brummell emphasized as the most important contribution of the scenario approach:

> When we first began using scenarios we tended to produce these wonderful books in which we took great pride. We thought of these books as being our product as being the real output of what we were trying to do. It was only after a period of time that we began to realize that these books really didn't matter, that what we were really trying to do is to get people thinking about the future and developing common visions. The real product was that process, getting everyone to develop a common understanding or map of the situations we might be facing, and increasing participation in the process both of creating those visions and of working at what we might do about them if they should come to pass.

At the same time, Brummell emphasized that the scenario approach, does not create a shared framework at the expense of narrowing vision or enforcing group-think. He argued that the other important element of the scenario approach is that it is premised on the process of acknowledging uncertainty (as Donald Michael had advocated) and on exploring different perspectives:

> . . . When you are looking at scenarios what you are trying to do is shift paradigms, consciously to get out of one simple logic that we use day-to-day to interpret things, and to think about or try out different logics that could be used to interpret what is happening. When you use a different logic or paradigm you can see a world in which a different set of variables become important.

> . . . Scenarios are totally different from forecasting in that scenarios treat uncertainty up front. You accept from the beginning that the future is unpredictable. . . . Scenarios move us away from the false certainty of forecasting approaches and instead make us concentrate on the risks involved and the alternate ways or alternate environments in which decisions may play out. Scenarios provide multiple pictures of the future as opposed to the single vision of a forecast.

> . . . when you use a forecasting approach the effect is to coverup uncertainty. The more uncertain things are the more the people involved in making the forecast talk to each other and effectively come up with a group-think solution, where in a sense you are protected by the fact that everybody is saying more or less the same thing. Scenarios challenge that approach. Scenarios explicitly demand that you look at alternative ways in which the story might unfold.

> That's why, for example, when the oil price collapsed in '86 Shell already had examined a scenario for a $15.00 a barrel oil price, and so we were much better prepared than the rest of the industry to do what needed to be done when that happened. It wasn't that we forecast that it would happen, it's that we examined the alternative possibilities in an uncertain environment, and so prepared ourselves to deal better with whatever occurred.

Brummell also underlined how the scenario approach helped to generate a shared language and common culture within Shell:

> . . . Scenarios also become a part of the language we use within the company, so that for example in one set of Shell Canada scenarios, we had one scenario called Cooperative Restructuring (CR) and another called Protective Nationalism (PN). And it would be quite common within the company during discussions on a number of matters to have people say that

something related to a CR world or that such and such would only happen in a PN world. Scenario titles become a shorthand for a whole complex array of ideas about the future and what they mean. They become very, very important for internal communication and for developing a common corporate view of the world.

Would the scenario approach work in government? According to Brummell:

I think it is much more difficult to do the sort of scenario work I have been discussing in governments: Their size and complexity is so much greater. Another important constraint in government is the fishbowl in which you operate. Any scenarios you spin internally are likely to become public, which is a considerable constraint in being able to think the unthinkable. But even with those constraints, it still seems to be essential and worthwhile to develop such approaches within the government for thinking about contingencies, for thinking about the future.

Some participants agreed:

I think the process that Arden was talking about earlier, when they go through the planning process with national company managers, translating objectives into plans and so on, is comparable to what goes on in a governmental planning process. The one difference is they begin not from a single implicit scenario about the future but rather try to make explicit alternate scenarios of how the future might unfold. One of those scenarios, as I understand it, is what they often refer to as the "business as usual" scenario, which corresponds to the sort of assumptions we tend to make in government when we begin a planning process: that the future will unfold in a certain fashion that is not too dissimilar from the present.

What I wonder is why it would not be possible to pursue a similar kind of process with Ministers, to lay out for them the alternate future scenarios and what the implications of the particular decisions that they are about to take would be under those different contingencies. What would be the impediments to trying something like that?

Others expressed scepticism about the viability of efforts to create a longer-term vision, given the realities of political timetables:

. . . senior civil servants really can't contemplate any scenario that is not relevant to the politicians, and the politicians inherently are focused on shorter-term planning that is very tied to the election cycle. So I wonder if the kind of system you are outlining really can be applied in its entirety to government given our built-in orientation towards a shorter-term political cycle?

But this was strongly countered by roundtable members who argued that failure to take a longer term view and to construct a shared vision was likely to increase political difficulties, and that it was a responsibility of the Public Service to provide Ministers with such a longer-term perspective:

> . . . if you aren't operating within a longer term vision those short-term tactical moves really don't get you very far. In the end you don't, and no one else does, understand what you are about. On the other hand once you have got some strategic direction, some vision of where you are going, then it is possible to act on a short-term basis but in a way that makes sense. So that whatever the political difficulties may be in trying to adopt something like a scenario or a longer term approach, it seems to me that if you don't do it the political difficulties are a lot greater. . . .

> ***

> . . . You know, maybe we are too easy on ourselves. We use, as officials, the fact that Ministers tend to approach things from a short-term political perspective to excuse the fact that we, as officials, don't do anything more. Maybe if we did more, if we tried to do some more long-term thinking, we would be in a position to present more options to the Minister. . . . Senior management of the department could have some more systematic process for looking at scenarios and other longer-term studies, and so could be able to present some of that to the Minister. . . . Right now most departments don't really give our Ministers that option.

Shared Information Systems

In addition to the scenario approach, the roundtable concluded that other techniques for generating a shared framework and interpretation needed to be explored. Amongst those would be computer-based approaches such as using simulations and a variety of graphic means to display information. Some of these were touched on in our discussions with executives at Canada Post, as well as in other sessions, but we did not have the time or resources to explore them further during the project. One partial exception was a case study that examined an effort to create a shared information system amongst several departments.

The case study told the story of the efforts of one department to develop a sophisticated information system that provided detailed information on Canada's defence-industrial base. It was designed to be used by a variety of departments as a tool in pursuing their own program responsibilities (for example in areas such as industrial development, defence policy and international trade). The system is built around a large database and overlaying that is a second level, which allows for manipulation of the data into complex patterns, and a system for presentation of the data in the form of reports and graphs in order to answer particular questions users might want to formulate. The system also is designed to encourage the exploration of scenarios and to enable the asking of "what-if" questions.

While the technology is impressive, in the end it was rejected by the user departments. Part of the reason for that rejection seemed to be that insufficient attention had been paid at the outset to developing a common language and framework, so that the user departments found it very difficult to integrate the results of the information system within their own frames (to translate the information into knowledge).

To be useful to those departments, the outputs needed to be translated, but to the extent the system managers sought to provide that translation, they were perceived to be competing with the user departments. In the words of the case study:

> The assumption we started with—that there is a close relationship between information and decision making—rests heavily on the rational actor model of political behaviour. That model assumes that all actors and their organizations are rational; that conflicting views, questions of jurisdiction, and so on are of slight consequence because information on its own merits points to solutions for the problem(s) at hand. We know now that our premise was simplistic.

... In retrospect, we held to the view that the availability of the information in itself had some intrinsic worth which could be recognized through better decision-making. We concentrated on designing a system that could manipulate in a number of different ways a broad range of data. ... However, we placed too much attention on technology and not enough on the human element.

The case study seemed to illustrate that the creation of a common language and framework is a precondition to making effective use of information systems. While the technology, by itself, cannot create it, once that framework is in place (as we saw in the case of Canada Post), the technology can be used to communicate, reinforce and build upon it. Participants felt that this also underlined once more the need to strengthen the strategic capabilities of government to generate those frameworks:

It seems to me that there are some general issues here which aren't being addressed yet. We have seen that one of the consequences of the information revolution is the capacity to create, maintain and link administrative databases in ways that were never available before. And, as we have seen, these raise a host of policy and management issues. But it also seems to me to raise an enormous array of opportunity. But if these opportunities are going to be reaped they have got to be planned, and it is clear from our discussion that that sort of planning function has got to be interdepartmental, it goes well beyond the mandate or the time horizon of any single department. . . . .

***

Yes, I think that's right and of course there are lots of issues that transcend the interest of one department, the health system, the justice system, the education system, and so on. These are enormous issues with enormous potential for designing systems that link capabilities across departments and allow information to be focused in a manner that can improve the quality of decision-making for the government as a whole. But currently the responsibility is spread here and there.

***

. . . I think an important recurring theme in our discussion of the implications of the information society, and not only today, has been the importance of developing, of regenerating, the strategic capacities of the system. That's even more important, in the context of the information society, than it was before.

Constructing a Shared Framework within Society

The Role of the Media

From the beginning of the project, we had recognized the growing role of the media as a central reality of the information society. The original project description had stated that in the information society:

> . . . the media plays a crucial role in shaping the policy agenda and determining which voices will be heard to the greatest effect. The interaction and mutual reinforcement amongst governments, various interests and the media, and the information or misinformation that results, become an increasingly important part of the process of governance. Government now means not just the administration of established functions, but the constant negotiation of coalitions with regions, with the private sector, with other nations, with special interest (or single issue) groups— all taking place in a noisy, information rich, increasingly media-centred public forum. . . .

The media play a central role in the process by which data and information is translated into knowledge within society overall. The media focus not so much on "news" as on "stories," on ways of organizing information into patterns that make sense, given their frameworks of interpretation. But because of the role and reach of the media, those frameworks are, perhaps, the mostly widely shared within society. To explore how this process works from the perspective of the media itself, the roundtable met with a panel of leading Canadian journalists: Elly Alboim, Peter Trueman and Hugh Winsor.

What they described to us was a profession undergoing a profound transformation and essentially becoming a market-driven, entertainment business. The most striking description they provided of that change deserves to be quoted at length:

> Journalism has begun . . . changing its assumptions and altering its test of relevance. It has done so without much discussion and with little accountability. It has allowed the market to help in that redefinition,

assuming that market forces are the ultimate form of accountability. But it continues to use outdated professional models to shelter it from public and regulatory scrutiny, allowing its clientele to assume the old models still govern its behaviour.

Some of the new assumptions and practices:

Journalists provide information people *want* to know. Information has to be interesting, entertaining and relevant.

Intrinsic importance is a less valuable concept than relevance. There has to be consumer impact, visible affect or effect, or clear implication for a story to be relevant.

Complex issues are difficult to understand and not immediately relevant. If they cannot be disregarded *a priori*—an increasingly problematic assumption—they must be made more manageable, redefined so they become more obviously relevant. One way of doing that is to personalize those issues. It is assumed that telling complex stories through the eyes of individuals or by individual example makes them easier to understand and, hence, more relevant. . . .

To be interesting and relevant, information on television, and increasingly in print, is transmitted through storytelling, adopting dramatic narrative to accomplish the transformation. This rewards conflict and denouement and begins to explain why event or decision are more understandable and newsworthy than process.

The fear of the audience not understanding or retaining information and, more importantly, of the audience choosing not to consume, has led to a simplification of language and story structure. It also justifies a simplification of fact presentation and a distillation of stories to their simplest elements. It has led to an emphasis on presentation skills on television and narrative skills in print.

The corporate culture operating within media demands adherence to this simplification and managers tend to hire and promote its advocates. It has taken on aspects of a theology and calls itself 'democratization of information.' It tends to disguise a creeping anti-intellectualism fostered, in part, by a generation of journalists who have not needed to understand complexity because their product is invariably reduced to a sum of the simplest common elements of any issue.

If an issue is too complex to be communicated easily by means of simplification or impervious to easy redefinition by means of personalization or demonstrating consumer impact, it can be dropped altogether. If that means consumers of information products don't get whole classes of information, so be it. There is a concurrent assumption that people who really have to know about these kind of issues have other ways of finding out.

To a certain extent, that is true. We have seen in Canada and the United States an increasing stratification of media. Because certain societal transactions can't fit within the new models and because certain groups require information about those transactions, elite media has been fostered to discuss them. News letters, specialized newspapers, public affairs television deal with classes of information and process that mass media do not. By definition, the mass of information clients do not receive this information. It is now possible to conduct certain activities in public and rest fully confident they will remain essentially private or at least limited to that community of interest involved in those activities.

In their very structure, television newscasts and newspapers redesign their hierarchy of information to reflect narrative style and to create more attractive packaging. In television, the advent of 'people meters' has meant that television producers now are able to read minute-to-minute tables to determine what kind of information and what sequences of information send viewers to the remote control buttons television producers fear so much. . . .

Ultimately what happens is that the established hierarchy of most important to least important disappears without the client quite realizing it. Since the nature of the cues wasn't apparently changed, what alters is peoples' sense of what is important. . . .

Some observations:

Because this is basically a framework, it probably is much too harsh. There is, of course, much variation and many more greys than admitted to above. Nevertheless some observations do emerge.

When you alter your editorial test from what do your clients need to what do they want, you may not serve them as fully as originally contemplated when the press won its protected independence.

People who rely on the mass media for most of their information end up with a highly skewed diet and issues that ultimately may be of crucial importance will not be well debated or understood.

There is an obvious trend towards the trivialization of public policy. Complex transactions are reduced to 'winners and losers' analysis; drama and conflict are artificially injected; option setting is perceived as decision-making because of impatience with process; national debate on options becomes political struggle, risk avoidance becomes a purpose in policy-making. Governance becomes, at least in part, an exercise in damage control and desensitization. And because of all this, media and policy-makers live in a climate of hostility, distrust and manipulation.

In effect what the panel of journalists was telling us was that the ways in which the media now tended to frame issues (for example focusing on conflict, on the short term, on winners and losers, on event and image and so on) was undermining the traditional canons of the profession, and was inimical to good governance. This was underlined in the course of the discussion:

Let's take another public policy example which has really major implications for concepts of country: free trade and Mexican free trade, it's an almost unmanageable issue from a public policy standpoint. How do you argue about structural change, how do you have an informed public discussion about job losses and so on, how do we get this into the public domain for a sensible discussion in the kind of environment that we have been discussing?

* * *

You have to be confident enough about the basic intelligence of the people out there over time, that they will get past the initial stories of this or that company closing down and understand the broader case. If in fact there is a good case, if it is strong, over time, it will permeate.

* * *

There has to be some way of desensitizing the issues. Everything can't be dealt with as though the government's future hangs in the balance. The Ministers should be allowed to make mistakes and we need to figure out how to create an environment that will allow for that. I think many of the problems that we are having in the country right now have to do with the absence of that. How do you create fair and accurate and desensitized information?

* * *

But as soon as you desensitize it, as soon as you remove the conflict, you remove the news value and then you are right back to the problem of how to get out the facts? If the story can't be phrased as a 'government hanging in the balance' issue, then you don't have a news story.

* * *

Well that points to the fundamental need to redefine what news is. We can't continue simply to cover traffic accidents and air crashes.

Some roundtable members argued that there was no choice but to learn to play that media game:

I remember a conversation I had with Marylou Findlay a couple of years ago. We were talking about public policy issues and she said well the problem with you is that you don't recognize that the world has gone from the oral to the visual, if you are going to deal with public policy issues you have got to deal with them in a visual sense. So I started to make a practice every time I moved to a new file to go through every newscast, journal tape and so on to get all of the images that people had seen on the subject. On the basis of that I then sat down to develop a communications strategy....

What I am trying to say, I suppose, is that we are in a kind of dance and that many of us learned to do the waltz, but now we are in this rock-'n-roll kind of dance with the media, and we don't either of us know how to get out of it. I don't think we feel that what we are doing is the best in terms of public policy, in terms of the public interest, and maybe it leads to crude manipulative leaders, but how do we get out of this kind of problem? Because now, in this town, if you want to deal with public policy, the bottom line is how would it play on the National, how would it play on the news tonight.

Others argued that was not good enough and that we needed to find better approaches in the interest of good governance:

We need to be able to move beyond this game. We are supposed to be looking at the information society and governance, we are talking about a whole new change in the way the world is working. Fundamental, systemic changes which don't make news. Both politicians and the media are locked into the old game.... But the real issue we need to address is one of changing value structures, the overall impact over time of changing value structures, and it is at that level that we can deal with the kind of questions we are talking about, and effect the kind of change that is going to bring about important shifts in our country and in the world. . . .

***

Well that's nice from a distance, but how do you take it down to the level of the issues that are in front of us bureaucrats, for example something like the Mexico Free Trade issue? In this case the issue is not whether you are going to lose jobs in Collingwood, the issue should be how our industry can compete with other industries in the North American market, and what we are going to do about that. And if your goal is to have an enlightened national debate about that, how do you use the media in that direction?

***

. . . I don't accept the view that you can't have a public debate about these sorts of questions. What's important, I think, is the way that you go about it. If you have a politician making colourful comments, comparing Newfoundland to Bangladesh for example, then the debate is likely to remain at that level. If the issue is introduced at a different level, say at a meeting of the Learned Societies next Spring, then you get a different level of discussion. It's interesting to see how corporate people inject their possible future strategies, when they want to get a debate going they don't call the *Globe and Mail*, instead they'll accept an invitation to speak to a financial analysts' society or something like that. That's the way to float ideas and to get them to develop at a different level of analysis and discussion. . . . Let it be discussed and debated at that level and let the information spread and be considered more calmly before it gets politicized.

The view also was expressed that we were in a transitional stage, and that as visual literacy increased, as a more visually literate generation came of age, we would find ways to use visual imagery and narrative structure to strengthen our capacity to govern ourselves. Roundtable members also noted the promise of interactive media, that would enable members of the public to participate more actively in the creation of shared frameworks of interpretation. As Peter Trueman phrased it:

We should, perhaps, make a distinction not just between information and news, but between information and knowledge. Dr. Daniel Boorstin, formerly of the U.S. Library of Congress, made the point on television recently that with information systems like CNN, in which news is recycled and broadcast every half hour, information actually displaces knowledge. Knowledge has endured, Dr. Boorstin said, because it describes the world over generations, not day by day.

When citizens, by interacting with those in charge of input for their television screens and computers, actually engage in conversation with journalists and civil servants, knowledge may finally be restored to its rightful eminence. And the market for journalistic trivia, now a mainstay of the mass media, could be expected to diminish.

The Role of Interactive Technologies

To explore the potential of interactive technologies to foster public participation in governance, and in the construction of shared frameworks of interpretation, of shared knowledge, the roundtable met with Mary Ann Young, who had undertaken a major study on that issue for the U.S. Office of Technology Assessment. She began her presentation by situating interactive technologies in the context of other, more established, forms of public participation:

> ... Obviously voting is one way of participating, but a vote does not convey a lot of information to government. When I vote for somebody it doesn't really tell them what I like or don't like about their policies, and the number of people that I have to choose from is so limited anyway.
>
> Another way of participating is through interest groups, which are becoming much more important. Their growing influence is partially due to information technology, which facilitates their fundraising and communications activities through mechanisms like direct mail, desktop publishing, use of the mass media and so forth. But we have so many interest groups involved in the process now, that they almost seem to cancel each other out. So the real effectiveness of interest groups is open to question and, perhaps more importantly, individuals who don't belong to an interest group may be cut out of the system.
>
> Opinion polls are another method of at least indirect participation, and (again due to technologies) polls now can be taken almost instantaneously. Polls clearly are having a very strong influence on government, although whether that is good or bad is debatable. There are serious questions about the kind of information we get from opinion polls, it's almost impossible to design survey questions that aren't biased in some ways, and further bias results from the ways in which the questions are asked (over the phone, or in person) and so on. So again, it's a limited channel for participation in decision-making.

Until recently, information technology essentially was used for one-way communication from the government to the people. There was very little happening in the way of interactive use of technologies to communicate to government. But more recently a few very promising experiments have got underway. . . . There are a growing number of computer-based communications systems in the U.S. and they are just starting to be used in governance. So far, more of these systems are being used as databases, to allow people to get on and to search and find information. A lot of governments are beginning to set-up that sort of thing. . . .

But at the local level, a lot more is going on related to broader questions of governance. First, an increasing amount of administrative activities are being handled on-line; for example, enabling people to apply for a license or a permit electronically and having that issued much more quickly and cheaply than would be the case using older methods. We also are beginning to see the establishment of terminals in shopping malls and schools and libraries.

I think that we will see these systems increasingly used to foster public policy discussion over the next 10 years . . . more towns and cities and governments and more people everywhere are experimenting with it, learning to use it, getting on networks, so that 10 years from now many of the technological and social barriers to using these systems likely will be eliminated. . . . Also 10 years from now a generation of kids who have grown up with computers will be part of the electorate and using these techniques to communicate with government will seem far more natural to them.

Some participants expressed concern about the effects that so interconnected a society might have: "It is relatively easy to manage a policy file when you can go out and talk to 20 people. That really won't work any more and now we have to go out and deal with hundreds of people. As that increases I think it does affect the capacity to govern." But others countered that:

... we don't really have much choice. More people are becoming involved with computers and a new generation of kids is growing up who are very comfortable using that technology, so that interacting through computers becomes increasingly a natural way to operate. At the same time, technologies are being advanced which will make computers more accessible, so that in the next generation machines will be far easier to use and connected to a much wider range of services more cheaply. That reality is coming in any case, and the issue for us is really what that means for the process of governance. How do we govern effectively in that more interconnected environment, with all of the possibilities and requirements for public participation that are likely to open up?

Many roundtable participants saw real opportunities for using the new interactive technologies, to foster public learning:

> One thing that this reminds me of is a proposal made at one of our earlier sessions about possibly using kiosks in public locations where people would be able to come in and interactively deal with simulations or scenarios on computers, ask what-if questions and see what the implications of various decisions might be. Then, as they come to better understand the choices and the implications, they could provide their input to government on the course of action they would prefer. That might provide a way both to educate the population and to elicit their views. . . .

> ***

> . . . it seems to me that there is some real potential to use these approaches more creatively. We have got to learn how to do that because a more interactively connected society is going to happen one way or another and so we need to figure out ways for it to happen that can facilitate effective governance. Also . . . when people become involved in these issues, they can start to understand them better and understand their implications. So one of the real potential benefits of moving in this direction would be the extent to which people will come to learn to understand the issues better. . . .

So for many participants, the interactive technologies could and should be used to facilitate a public learning process, a process of creating shared understandings, shared frameworks of interpretation, across society.

Conclusions

The process of transforming data and information into knowledge, the process of learning, appears to us to be central to governing in an information society. It involves constructing shared frameworks of interpretation in the context of which that information can be translated and made meaningful. As we have seen, in a variety of contexts, the roundtable concluded that the government needs to strengthen its capacity to lead the construction and renewal of those frames. That framing process is key both to the information-based ways of organizing discussed in Chapter 2, and to the ways of forging consensus in an information society discussed in Chapter 3. It is fundamental to effective leadership.

In this chapter we explored a variety of tools for doing that, including scenarios, developing within government a cadre of knowledge workers skilled at translating between communities of interpretation, making more strategic use of shared information systems to foster a shared perspective (as we had seen at Canada Post), using interactive technologies, and developing a different relationship with the media. These are by no means a comprehensive list of potential approaches but, taken together with suggestions in previous chapters, do offer promising starting points for further exploration.

In addition to particular tools, our discussions underlined a basic change in attitude and approach that seems to be required to deal with the new information environment. Both within and outside government, it was argued, it is self-defeating to try to control what data or information is released or available. The real challenge is to provide leadership to the continuing process by which people interpret and make sense of that information. For example, in dealing with the press it may be better to disburse information (data organized within a particular framework) on a more regular, open basis through briefings, so that they can better understand the context within which decisions are being made. As one member of the roundtable put it:

> ... The reality is that [information] is going to come out in any case, so the issue is to put it out in a context that makes it comprehensible and useful in developing an understanding and discussion of the issues. The Americans are ahead of us in this new understanding. You can't protect information, but what you can do is put forward your interpretation as effectively as possible. If you don't do that, then someone else's interpretation, be it a special interest group or somebody else, will be how that information is understood.

Whether dealing within the government apparatus or more broadly within society, effective leadership increasingly depends on the ability to lead that process by which (in Harlan Cleveland's formulation) data and information are translated into knowledge. We will return to this in our concluding chapter.

5

Conclusions

After over two years of investigation, we are concluding that the changes that were initially described as flowing from the "transition to an information society" are even more fundamental, and far-reaching in their effects, than had been suspected at the beginning.

As society becomes more interconnected, complex and turbulent, more traditional ways of organizing and governing are being overwhelmed. In a more educated, interconnected, information-rich environment, governing systems predicated on a limited flow of information, including both bureaucracy and representative democracy itself, lose their credibility and authority. Unless those systems can adjust themselves to the realities of the information society, that process of overload and fragmentation, which we are witnessing in Canada and around the world, will continue and accelerate.

This point was underlined strongly at one of our concluding roundtables, when we broke into smaller groups to consider what should be included in the conclusions of the project. One group of participants noted:

> ... that in ... crisis situations the system at large had failed to function, had lost its capacity to be sufficiently nimble and equipped to deal with an information age, to deal with the kinds of issues that increasingly will face government. That was a very strong conclusion that emerged from this exercise. Our old ways of organizing simply will not work in the environment into which we are moving.

Another group of roundtable members, working independently, expressed a similar view:

> We concluded that a major point to emphasize in our conclusion is that it is very questionable that the institutions and instincts that we have inherited are adequate to enable us to be nimble enough to respond to the

complexities of the issues that we are facing in the 1990s. The structures of government tend to be rigid and antiquated, but I guess our feeling was that it wasn't just a question of structures. In a period of rapid change, structures may be less important. A particular structure is likely to be outdated by the time it goes through the long process of organizational change. Instead we need to focus more on behaviour and on the generation of shared understandings, in the context of which we might be able to organize ourselves more flexibly around issues.

And in the view of participants these changes are not temporary or cyclical, but represent a fundamental system change:

Some people argue that we are in a pendulum swing, at the far right end of the swing, and that things will gradually move back towards the centre, and as that happens the legitimacy of governments again will increase. The other argument, though, is that the nature of the system has changed so much that government, as it has operated in the past, simply cannot cope with the complexity of the information society, and so its role needs to be rethought. I tend to be more in the latter camp. . . . There are deeper issues. . . .

***

Yes, and if we take the analogy of the way in which business has been restructuring, with the removal of a lot of middle management, we also may be looking at the removal of a lot of levels of government. If you look at Europe, for example, you can ask to what extent do we need nation-states, are they going to be breaking up into smaller units that then associate in larger regional markets? We are seeing a lot of change going on . . .

***

. . . In some areas the role of government may be becoming irrelevant, while in others that role is changing dramatically. For example, look at the billions of dollars that are traded everyday on computers. There is a massive capital movement going on between countries all around the world. What Department of Finance can hang on to that?

Governing effectively in this new environment will require fundamental innovation. As we have outlined in the last three chapters, those innovations will need to include finding ways to enhance the learning capacity of our governing systems by developing new ways of:

- organizing within government;
- . forging consensus amongst the proliferating number of players in the information society; and
- using information to support the new ways of organizing and consensus-building.

This is as huge an undertaking as it is vital. In the project we only have begun to examine these issues and to explore which innovations, which new ways of integrating, are most likely to be effective in the information society. While in the last few chapters we have outlined a number of ideas that we believe merit further attention, in the next section of this concluding chapter we would like to reiterate those that we believe should be at the top of the list.

We will include in that list (as we have throughout the report) only those conclusions that are applicable across government or, even more broadly, across society. Conclusions that are applicable to individual departments (for example those contained in the case studies undertaken for the project) have been communicated separately to those departments by the appropriate member of the roundtable.

A Map for Further Exploration

In our initial explorations, we have found a recurring theme, which seems applicable both to issues of organizing and of governing; namely the need to pay far more attention to defining the context, to framing the issue, to specifying the objectives, the parameters and process, and then to let the relevant players (for example, from various sectors of society on questions of governance, or from an agency's staff members when it comes to questions of organizing) have as much freedom as possible to innovate new approaches and learn more effective ways to achieve those objectives.

One adage that was repeated often in our discussions was that while the Japanese argue endlessly over ends, once a conclusion is reached implementation is swift and effective, resting on a well-forged consensus and widely shared understanding about what is being attempted. In North America, by contrast, the tendency is to assume we agree on the ends and, instead, to argue endlessly about the means (which, in effect, becomes a not very effective surrogate for discussing the broader questions of objectives and values that we have ignored or bypassed).

What is becoming increasingly clear, as societies become more interconnected and as the number of players in the process of governance multiply, is that we need to invest more time and attention in developing a shared understanding of where we want to go, in a more systematic process of agenda-setting. Such a shared framework is the essential context that can allow the multiplying players in the governance process mutually to coordinate their actions.

The development and continual evolution of that strategic framework, of that learning environment, is an essential part of effective governance in an information society. It may well be that, in the information society, the direct role of government in the delivery of services (as we saw in Chapter 2), and in more traditional forms of regulation (as we saw in Chapter 3), will diminish. But that will not diminish the responsibility of government to find appropriate ways to ensure that the public interest is protected and that public goods are provided. To do that will require government to enhance its capacity to play a framework role.

Another way of looking at this derives from the understanding that one of the basic dilemmas of the information society is not so much an overload of data or information as it is a deficit in our capacity to frame and interpret that data and information, to translate it into useful knowledge. From that perspective, an essential skill in the information society is the ability to develop shared ways of interpreting, to construct a shared context within which we better can organize and govern ourselves. It is that skill that we have come to see as central to effective leadership in the information society.

Often, in the project, this ability to generate shared interpretations was discussed in terms of the capacity to create shared myths, shared stories:

> It seems to me that an important point in all of this, in converting information into knowledge, is to tell a story. The ability to tell a story in a convincing way is becoming a key skill for governance, as Ronald Reagan illustrated. Increasingly, the mythology-creating ability, the ability to simplify and to communicate effectively at the front end, is essential. Part of the problem with unity is that we are not dealing with a story, but with a bureaucratic proposal that has lots of detail. There are too many points. As Sylvia Ostry said, what you really need are two or three points knitted together in a story that people can deal with.
>
> ***
>
> I think you are right that it is essential to have the story up front, and that goes back to the adage about the importance of selling a question before you can sell an answer. You need, in a sense, to provide that story-line as a context and, in that context, you then can spin out all kinds of sub-themes, which are made meaningful to people through the medium of that story. Ronald Reagan was extremely successful in doing that, while Jimmy Carter, although he knew an awful lot more about the details of government, couldn't tell a story to save his life. . . . There was no sense of a clear vision that somehow pulled all of this stuff together, no story that people could identify with and use to internalize all that information as knowledge.

If government is going to be able to lead the development of shared frameworks of interpretation, of shared agendas, in effect to lead a process of societal learning, changes will be needed both within government and in the relation between government and other players in the governance system. Those changes will be as difficult to achieve as the task is essential. To that end, amongst the ideas and conclusions generated by the project, we especially would underline the following issues for further attention and more detailed development.

Constructing a Shared Perspective across Government

Within government, members of the roundtable emphasized that most issues in the information society now extend beyond the mandate of any one department and beyond the time horizon of most governmental planning. In a sense, the boundaries (both in space and in time) within which we operate correspond less and less with the boundaries of the issues that need to be addressed. That creates institutional impediments to comprehending the very issues on which government most needs to provide leadership.

Participants felt that there is a need to enhance the capacity to develop a government-wide perspective on these issues and to organize effectively around them. The challenge is to find a way to do that without creating the heavy bureaucratic costs that previous efforts at coordination have engendered:

> Over the years we have seen a continual struggle between decentralization and centralization, trying to find the right balance. We all know the history of Ministries of State, and Cabinet Committees, and so on. If it is the case, as it is alleged at least in the private sector, that the information revolution puts a premium on nimbleness and quickness of foot and that, therefore, bureaucratic hierarchy is stultifying and too slow, it seems to me that raises the question of centralization-decentralization again in a new way. On the one hand we have the need to reflect the interrelatedness of issues in the way in which we operate, but, at the same time, in order to foster nimbleness, there is a premium on decentralizing government activity.

> So how do you capture the interrelatedness of those issues without creating the elaborate hierarchies we have seen in the past or "presidentializing" the Prime Minister? That seems to me to be a central dilemma of how we organize ourselves in the information society. . . .

> ***

> We need to develop more effective structures for interdepartmental collaboration to address these questions, and find ways to do that without generating the kinds of bureaucratic costs which previous efforts in that direction have generated. Some clues of how to proceed in that regard have come up in our discussions and also can be suggested by the nature of the information revolution itself.

Amongst the ideas that we have explored in that regard have been the development of techniques to organize around issues rather than just functions, the use of scenario-planning approaches, the construction of shared information systems, and developing the skills and the ethic that Donald Michael has summarized as "the new competence." Central to all of those is the need to foster a shared, longer-term, strategic perspective, in the context of which, particular questions can be addressed more effectively both within government and more broadly within society.

The Public Service as a Learning Organization

We also underlined that in the information society, as one group of participants phrased it toward the end of the project: "we need to understand the role of government and of public servants as being essentially one of knowledge workers rather than just problem solvers." Another group of roundtable members elaborated the point:

> . . . when we talk about the problems of governing in an information society, what we are fundamentally addressing is the fact that we have not found a way, within government, to take information and translate it and develop it, either for our own internal purposes or for purposes of dealing with external constituencies. What it comes down to is that we need more people, and I guess they are knowledge workers, people who can take a whole bunch of information, share it within the system and outside the system, and turn it into something that becomes digestible and useful by ourselves as bureaucrats and by Canadians.

We need to work through how to develop Public Servants whose primary role is understood to be that of knowledge workers (skilled in the process by which data and information is translated into knowledge, and by which shared frameworks of interpretation are created), and the implications of that for questions such as recruitment, training, promotion, methods of management and so on. As one participant phrased it: ". . . we're in the process of converting from a system populated by a bunch of very transactional people who do routine things, and are moving instead to giving them tools to take the routine off their desk and to free them to do value-added work, and we need to develop the capacity to provide that value-added."

More broadly, participants recognized that what was required was a basic change in the culture and practices of the Public Service, the development of the Public Service as a learning organization or society. One step in that direction has been recent efforts to introduce Total Quality Management (TQM) techniques within government. But much more is needed. If government is to provide the sort of leadership needed in the information society, it will require the support of a different sort of Public Service, one that is more attuned to change, more able to learn and adapt flexibly to a turbulent environment, more able to address longer-term issues that cut across departmental boundaries. This means strengthening the learning capacity of the Public Service, and finding better ways to engage other sectors of society in that learning process.

Sharing Knowledge as the Key to Effective Leadership

Another strong conclusion was the extent to which, in the information society, the sharing of knowledge and interpretations, rather than the hoarding of information, is the key to effective leadership:

> . . . in a sense, what we are seeing is an inversion of the old dictum that 'knowledge is power.' Today, by contrast, it seems that the propensity is to get out and share the knowledge as a basis for building coalitions for action. And that is quite a reversal of past practices that used to be followed in government and, indeed, in most human organizations, where the husbanding of information was used to give people bargaining or other power.

> ***

> That's right and the question then becomes . . . not whether you have [information] but what you use it for and how you interpret it. It is not the

data or the information that count, it is the interpretation or the knowledge, and the capacity to do that kind of interpretation and knowledge creation.

***

So, if I understand you, what you are saying is that the problem with the free trade debate or with Meech Lake, for example, is that Canadians were faced with what they perceived to be a government trying to control the information being dribbled out.... And the counter argument being made here is that it would have been in the government's interest to put out far more information to people to help in the creation of a common knowledge base, which would have provided the grounds for a more productive debate and a wider understanding.

***

Yes, and the current Constitutional conferences being held around the country may demonstrate, in an embryonic way, that that sort of approach can work.

What constitutes effective governmental leadership of that sort of more open societal learning process was a recurring issue throughout the project:

One of the conclusions I draw . . . is that there exists a capacity [on the part of the public] that we simply don't grasp and that, given the right structures of public investment to make information available and accessible, the general population is capable of taking on board and reasoning through a wide range of complex issues. That goes far beyond anything we have imagined or tried to do. It seems to me that we need to find ways to provide the information that people require, to feed that capacity to address these issues and that, if we don't do that, we face further alienation from government and a further breakdown in the governance process.

***

. . . I would be very leery of using the notion that the populace is capable of integrating these issues as an excuse to abdicate the leadership role government needs to play. It is not enough to say that we can put the information out and the knowledge somehow will develop, a more proactive role needs to be played, involving both governments and experts on given subjects.

***

I think government can play a leadership role (or not), whether you are dealing with the general public or just with elites. Government can play an active or a passive role in either case. If government sits back, in an interaction with three or four special interest groups and allows them to set the agenda, that is as much an abdication of leadership as what you are describing in the case of dealings with the public. On the other hand, there can be a role for government to play, a leadership role, in helping the public (or elites) to address these issues, in providing them with the information and other resources they require, and in leading the process of developing a common understanding and even a consensus.

Earlier in the project (outlined in Chapter 3) we heard presentations from Arthur Kroeger and Steven Waldhorn that detailed more or less successful efforts to develop such consensus-building efforts. We also explored Harlan Cleveland's model of how such processes operate, and examined the role of government in framing the issues and providing leadership to the overall process. But generally our sense is that we still have far to go in developing the government's capabilities to provide leadership to such a societal learning process:

> An awful lot of the approaches that have been discussed here seem to have more to do with how to neutralize interest groups, or how to get them on-side, in a sense dealing with the consensus process as a sort of damage control. I think an important question for us is whether that's the right way to think about this challenge, and whether we might be losing strategic opportunities to govern more effectively by taking the consensus-building process more seriously. I think we need to come back to a discussion of what those opportunities might be. . . .

> I would argue that consensus is really a process rather than an outcome, and that consensus is constantly being constructed. In Canada, I don't think we are very good at that, at least not recently, but if government is going to play the kind of leadership role we are discussing, I think it is essential that it engage in an effective consensus process.

> . . . the extent to which we tend to talk about consultation and consensus in the country right now is a symptom that we are not doing it very well. What we talk about as consultation these days doesn't have to do with an ongoing process of getting our act together as a range of players in society, and pointing ourselves in some direction. Other societies seem to do that a lot better. . . .

Using Information Technology to Foster Societal Learning

Another conclusion to be underlined is that interactive information technologies could be used to help to foster that sort of societal learning process, to help to generate and to sustain shared frameworks of interpretation. We need to investigate better ways of doing that:

> For example, it seems possible to take the system of national accounts, which have tyrannized the world for 40 years, and generate instead much more interesting data sets (satellites) that show how the world really works. One example is the Statistics Canada social policy simulation model, and others could be created for education, health, environment and so on. I wonder whether the fact that we haven't gone through that kind of process of public involvement and building familiarity with the implications of policy questions, might explain some of the problems we have run into with the goods and services tax. Such simulation models increasingly can be used to stimulate and inform public debate, and may prove to be indispensable in dealing with policy issues that have become so interconnected and complex.

Essentially, the idea would be to provide members of the public (as well as decision-makers from government and from other sectors of society) with access to a shared database and simulation models that could be used to explore the implications of different policy options. The players could use the models to ask "what-if" questions and to develop a shared understanding of the issues and of the options that were available, in effect to be involved in a shared learning process. That sort of learning process might be reinforced further by using the communications capabilities of the technology to foster electronic town hall meetings and the like.

To the degree that a shared interpretation of the issues and of the implications of the various policy options could be achieved, there would be a greater possibility of moving toward a workable consensus. This appeared to us to be one promising way in which the new technologies might be used to foster more effective governance.

In the same context, it was underlined that there is a public goods component to information and information technology:

... we also need to address the whole issue of the best ways in which the public can access data, information and knowledge, and what the public sector's role is in that game. As the number of channels of communication multiply through this revolution that we have all been talking about, it seems to me that we need to spend more time thinking about what the public interest is in marshalling that massive capacity to serve . . . [the public good].

We have licensed and entitled all kinds of special interests to become involved in the provision of data, information and knowledge, but we have not described a public function to provide for distribution of information, data and knowledge in the public interest. . . . we need to have a public policy to foster public awareness and public literacy. There ought to be new forms of public vehicles that permit access to the sea of knowledge in the world. . . .

Terra Incognita

The last few pages have indicated a number of ideas that we believe particularly merit further attention to strengthen the capacity of the public service to provide Ministers with the support they will require to govern and to lead effectively in an information society. Other ideas worthy of attention also are listed in the preceding three chapters. In the project we have had a chance only to begin to open up these questions and to begin to understand the terms in which they might be addressed. At one of our concluding roundtables, one participant summarized the point we had reached in understanding the implications for governance of the information society:

... while the old ways of doing things are being superseded by many of these changes, it's far from clear what the best new ways of doing things are. In some respects the role of government needs to be redefined, and in other respects government will need to develop smarter ways of doing some of the same things it has done before. In either case, I think we will be involved in rethinking the role of government, and in paying more attention to the issues of managing knowledge and generating shared frameworks of understanding.

> Perhaps a lot of the stuff government has done directly in the past now might be handled in different ways. But that does not diminish the fact that there is a need for something called a governance system, that there is a need for something called government, and that there is something called public goods. But in the information society, the role of government within the governance system is changing, as is our understanding of what public goods are and how best they can be provided.

Clearly it would take a more massive effort, involving a wider range of participants, to address these issues more systematically. In addition to those questions that we have placed on the agenda in this report, there are an even greater number of questions that have come up in our discussions which we have not had the time or resources to address even in a preliminary way. Examples of these include:

- developing more effective public/private partnerships;
- dealing with the power of images;
- developing feedback and accountability systems that allow us to learn more systematically from experience;
- issues of access to information and privacy;
- more effective ways to organize collective decision-making;
- ways to encourage risk-taking, creativity and critical thinking within the system;
- and more.

As well, given the limitations of our existing conceptual frames (as we discussed in the introductory chapter), no doubt other important questions will arise that we do not yet have the understanding even to ask.

A Continuing Process of Learning

As the project drew to a close, the members of the roundtable reflected on the value of the process we have been through over the last two years. One of the objectives of the project has been to test the value of this sort of process (participatory action research) in helping to develop more effective ways to understand and to deal with the crisis in governance that we now face. Participants strongly expressed the view that the experience has been very worthwhile. In the words of a report made by one group of participants to the roundtable:

> . . . this has been a unique learning experience for all of us, and we have all benefited from exposure to evolving new ideas and awareness of the topic of informatics and the information society, and have learned from that experience ways we can apply to our own particular work environments. . . . The value of exchanging ideas, of the case studies, of research and interpersonal discussion about these issues and about how they affect what each of us is doing, all of that was of very great value.

Another group, in agreeing with that view, added that there would be real benefit in spreading such a process more widely within the Public Service:

> . . . within the Public Service at the moment there needs to be more opportunities at the middle and senior management levels to embrace the interrelated character of modern public policy. There are insufficient structures within the Public Service at the moment, both formal and informal, to accomplish this, and this roundtable has provided an invaluable opportunity for that kind of process. Quite apart from the benefits derived with respect to the particular topics, there has been a very great value in providing a forum where Assistant Deputy Ministers can get together in a semi-formal process to examine broader issues.

Roundtable members also listed a number of characteristics that the experience of the last two years had demonstrated were essential to an effective learning process, including:

- continuity of membership;
- a neutral forum;
- participants attending in their own right, not representing the views of a department; and
- an ongoing secretariat to organize and support discussions and to provide regular feedback and project coordination.

Generally, roundtable members concluded that they would like to see the process continue beyond the life of the project, incorporating those essential characteristics. That continuing process might focus on more detailed examination of some of the questions raised by the project, as well as continuing the broader exploration needed to make sense of the fundamental changes in governance that are underway. There also was agreement that it would be desirable to include a wider range of participants in such a process than it had been possible to include within the project.

The roundtable suggested that, given its mandate, the Canadian Centre for Management Development (CCMD) would be the best home for such an effort within the government. Such an effort would be a natural and valuable extension of the work already undertaken by CCMD, and the incremental costs would be relatively small.

There also would be value in housing such an effort in an independent agency such as the IRPP, which already has had the experience of this project, and has the additional flexibility (and perceived neutrality) of being at arms length from government. Given the ways in which the number of players in the governance process are multiplying in the information society, it would be valuable to include more non-governmental participants and perspectives in any continuing process, and an independent agency could play an especially helpful role in that regard.

Members of the roundtable suggested that, in addition to publishing the final report, special efforts should be made to make Deputy Ministers aware of the findings of the project. Participants concluded that it also would be valuable, as another way of continuing the process, to pursue the idea of organizing a conference or two around these issues. One possibility would be a conference in Canada with people from other governments and other sectors of society, organized by the IRPP. Another would be an international conference with colleagues from other governments, perhaps organized under the auspices of the Organization for Economic Co-operation and Development (OECD).

More broadly, we believe that the ultimate success of this project should be judged by the extent to which it is not an end, but a beginning, the beginning of a more systematic search to develop new ways of governing appropriate to an information society. We have only begun to map this territory. We hope to see the process continued in greater depth and with the involvement of a broader range of participants.

In microcosm, the project itself exemplifies the sort of learning effort required for effective governance in a turbulent environment. It was designed to bring together officials from a variety of departments to explore issues that transcend the boundaries of any single department and the usual time horizon of governmental planning and decision-making. It was designed to explore the changing context of governance and to begin to build a shared understanding, a shared framework, amongst the participants. Even more important, it was designed to foster a continuing process of constructing such frameworks, a continuing process of learning to make sense of and to cope with more turbulent environments.

To do that, it adopted a participatory action research approach, bringing together researchers and practitioners from various sectors of society, and moving back and forth between broader theoretical discussion and efforts to apply those emerging insights in case studies of actual issues being faced by particular departments. This process has been undertaken in a neutral setting, has drawn on the insights of outside experts and representatives of various sectors of society, and has been built around a systematic process of feeding back insights gained in roundtable discussions to participants, and helping participants to use that feedback to steer their own cumulative learning process.

The process of governing in an information society, as we have come to understand it, needs to be conceived as an ongoing process of learning, a process of learning both within the government and, more broadly, within society. A continuing reality of the information society will be that the lifespan of particular instruments of governing will be limited. To deal effectively with such a rapidly changing environment, we need to become far more effective at developing new ways of governing appropriate to new circumstances. This project has been one example and (we hope) one beginning of the sort of ongoing learning process that will be required to underpin governing in an information society.

Part II

Selected Papers Presented to the Roundtable

Introduction to Part II

Throughout the project, the work of the roundtable was stimulated and focused by presentations made by a wide range of international authorities on issues pertinent to governing in an information society. A number of those authorities agreed to develop those presentations into more formal papers, which are presented here.

The discussions those presentations sparked are outlined in the report of the roundtable. The first two presentations, by Harlan Cleveland and by Donald Michael, were perhaps the most influential in the project, and references to them recur throughout the report and, in particular, in the first three chapters. The presentation by Steven Waldhorn was central to the discussion of experience with consensus-building described in Chapter 3, while the presentations by Peter Trueman on the media, and by Mary Ann Young on interactive technologies, helped to shape the discussions of those topics reported in Chapter 4.

In some cases, those discussions tracked fairly closely the issues raised in the presentations, while in others the presentations triggered more wide-ranging examinations, and elicited from the resource people insights not contained in their papers. Generally, I think it is fair to say that the resource people also learned from their involvement in the discussions of the roundtable. Certainly, developing that sort of mutual learning process was something we tried to foster throughout the project.

Of course, much more was presented to the project than is included in Part II. A number of the outside authorities who made valuable presentations to the roundtable were not in a position to turn their presentation into a more formal paper. There also were a wide range of previously published books and articles that were very influential in the work of the roundtable, which are not reproduced here. Finally, the departmental case studies, prepared by each participant and presented to the roundtable, remain with those Departments, for whatever additional use or dissemination they wish to undertake. In sum, the papers presented in Part II represent a small but important sample of the presentations made to the roundtable, and provide valuable additional insight into many of the issues that the project was designed to address.

"Safe for Diversity":
The Challenge of Governing in an Information Society

Harlan Cleveland*

Playwright Vaclav Havel, while he was president of Czechoslovakia, was asked on U.S. public television for his opinion, as a dramatist, of the 1989 histrionics in Eastern Europe. "It was," he replied with unrehearsed elegance, "a drama so thrilling and tragic and absurd that no earthling could have written it."

Since the drama of Tiananmen, we've been agog at each day's volcanic eruptions in the public squares and private chancelleries of four continents. We still are hardly more than spectators. Yet, as Shirley Hufstedler said, we've been like Emerson's elderly Boston gentleman who insisted on being awakened every ten minutes from his after dinner naps to hear the latest news.

The idea of political choice is "busting out all over." The big turnabout probably has been produced less by the political persuasion of the Western democracies than by their economic example. The root causes seem to be the inherent tendency of information to leak, plus the inherent attractiveness of such basic human notions as fairness, human rights, and government by consent of the governed. We're living in The Age of Choice. The right to choose may prove to be the dominant metaphor of the 1990s.

---

* Harlan Cleveland is Professor Emeritus of Public Affairs and Planning at the University of Minnesota's Hubert H. Humphrey Institute of Public Affairs. His long and distinguished career has included service as United States Assistant Secretary of State, Ambassador to NATO, Dean of the Maxwell School of Citizenship and Public Affairs, President of the University of Hawaii and Director of the Aspen Institute Program in Public Affairs. He currently serves as President of the World Academy of Art and Science. The latest of his ten books are *The Knowledge Executive: Leadership in an Information Society* and *The Global Commons: Policy for the Planet*. His new book, scheduled for publication in March 1993, is *Birth of a New World: An Open Moment For International Leadership*.

It's time now to start digesting. Herewith half a dozen spoonfuls of fibre to speed the process.

1. We've seen and felt two contrasting and colliding urges: top-down reform and the bubbling of political choice from below.

   Both the Soviet and Chinese strategies of reform-from-within are revolutions promoted—and, their leaders hoped, managed—from the top. In Eastern Europe there was some hasty top-down reform under the duress of placard-waving crowds. The lesson from all three cases is that top-down reform will always be too little and too late; "the people" will all too easily get out ahead of the reformers.

   The bubbles of political choice rose and choked the old leaders of Eastern Europe. In the Soviet Union, Mikhail Gorbachev, master of the fast break, kept having to adjust to a reform spirit (and a spirit of self-determination, in Lithuania and elsewhere outside of "Russia") that developed a life of its own.

   In China a tight little group of lifetime associates, friends and relations hangs on; but a prudent oddsmaker would now take bets, not on whether they will succeed but on when they will be pushed into oblivion.

2. It is hard to think of a time in world history when the political leaders of powerful nations have seemed so irrelevant to important outcomes. Well-known names—presidents and prime ministers of the world's military powers and economic powerhouses—have been staring at the evening news with ill-concealed astonishment. The "people power" cavorting on the world stage in 1989-90 had remarkably little to do with the customary measures of power: weapons, armies, gross economic product. More than anything else, the power of ideas has been in play.

3. The crowds were moved not by distant visions of Utopia, but by spreading information about neighbours who were obviously getting more goods and services, more fairness in their distribution, and firmer guarantees of human rights than their own bosses and planners were able to deliver.

What caught up with the rulers of China was unstoppable knowledge, especially among the educated young, of what was going on in Japan, South Korea, Taiwan, Hong Kong and Singapore. What caught up with the Communist leaders in Eastern Europe was what went on in the democracies of Western Europe. What turned the Soviet Union around was the growing perception, across the country and inside the leadership, that "catching up" even with a troubled America was a losing race.

Gorbachev kept saying that somehow, in one way or another, we have got to mobilize our own people's sense of political enthusiasm and economic hustle by setting them free from the anxiety and apathy that come with governance by secret informers and economic planners.

4. The toughest dilemma such top-down reformers face is how to educate their people, especially their young people, without luring them into dissidence. When it comes to politics, people who *think* are notoriously ornery and inventive. It doesn't seem to matter much what they have been trained to think *about*; part of what they learn in every field of knowledge is the joy of creative choice. If the freedom to choose is essential to their specialist learnings, it's no big step to the conviction that freedom of political choice is not only attractive but also attainable.

5. The top-down reformers keep trying to draw a line between safe and unsafe learnings. Pierre Perrolle, a former science counsellor at the U.S. embassy in Beijing, says that a century ago imperial China distinguished between "China's learning for essential matters" and "Western learning for practical matters." This dilemma is, he says, that: "China needs the practical learning from abroad, but how does one distinguish the practical from the essential?"

Especially when the practical is so essential. A good deal of Western culture comes packaged with the "practical" imports. Embedded in modern science and technology are Western notions about limits to government, about freedom to discover and experiment and innovate, about workers' rights, about managers leading without being bossy.

6. What is the lesson for Americans—and, I would hope, for Canadians—in the 1990s? Let's not cuddle up too close to reluctant reformers who are slated nearly everywhere for early retirement. Let's bet instead on the power of democratic contagion, interacting with the bubble-up power of political choice.

I may be a little closer to Canadian thinking than most Americans—not just because of Minnesota's geography, but because the public radio network in our part of the country exposes us to a good deal of news and commentary originating in Canada. Even so, I have no clear picture of Canadian reaction to this "open moment" in world affairs.

So, in preparation for our evening together, I tried to play a "let's pretend" game: Suppose I *were* Canadian, what would I expect my country to be thinking and doing about the Great Turnabout? My act of presumption (in both senses of that word) lasted only long enough for me to ask myself a puzzling question: What is the essence of being Canadian, and how does that identity relate to the tectonic shifts in world affairs just now?

Canada is an Experiment in Democracy

Canada is a remarkably successful effort to reconcile three traditions of political culture—British, French, American—and make a polity that is more than the sum of its parts. When a Chinese student tells a reporter in Tiananmen Square that he doesn't quite know what democracy is but he's sure China needs more of it, does he mean —

should he mean—that China needs more of what Canada already has? What have Canadians learned about living and working together that is uniquely exportable to those who think democracy works better for people than whatever they themselves have been enduring?

I can't answer that question for Canada, or even for the United States. But I think there are some universals in our democratic learnings. They come clothed not as an ideology for leaders to debate, but as a mindset for citizens of a free society:

- Democracy is a sense of community, not on everything or even on most things, but on a very few essentials: that it will be best if we don't settle scores by killing each other, that diversity of peoples and opinions is a Good Thing, that no child should go to bed hungry.
- Democracy is the idea that people can agree to take next steps together if they don't feel that they must first agree on *why* they are agreeing.
- Democracy is the expectation that, as a matter of course, the people will latch onto new ideas before their formal leaders do.
- Democracy is a system in which no one person or group or class or race or creed gets to say, with authority, what democracy is.

You have been looking at this puzzle—what is democracy and why does it work when it does?—through the prism of your personal and national experience. So your formulation is almost bound to differ somewhat from mine. But if people in Eastern Europe, Latin America, Asia and Africa are opting for democracy because they perceive us in the "West" as freer and more prosperous than their own institutions have made it possible for them to be, don't we "Westerners" have some obligation to try to distill the essence of what we have learned about making free institutions work? If we are (like it or not) a "city upon a hill," we had better understand what it means to govern ourselves as efficiently, as fairly, and as democratically as possible. For tonight, let's take Canada as the prism through which to view the essence of democracy.

Canada is an Experiment in "Uncentralization"

The initiative on most matters rests, in Canada, not with central authorities but with others, sometimes many others—with the provinces, with public corporations (which seem to be government-owned but don't seem to have to act like it), with private firms, with private citizens organized for all sorts of public purposes. In the United States we have a federal system too, with all residual powers reserved to the states; but our state officials wouldn't dream of asserting the policy control, for example over resources, that is taken for granted in some Canadian provinces.

New constitutions will now be written in two dozen countries or more, dealing with the degree to which highly centralized powers will now be devolved, split up, even atomized in newly uncentralized systems. What relevant lessons have Canadians learned from experience about reconciling "bubble-up" initiative with central authority?

Canada is an Experiment in Mixing Markets with Planning

In the ex-communist countries, and in most of the developing world, the problem now or soon is to convert from failed government-owned and government-led economies to some other economic system that meets human needs and serves human purposes. It won't be "socialism", but it won't be "capitalism", either. It will be some new alchemy of public planning and private enterprise.

The theoreticians of both those 19th century doctrines fell short because they focused on who *owns* the means of producing *things*, rather than on who guesses most astutely about what and why and how to invent and produce and market goods and services that consist mostly of knowledge. In the global knowledge society, information (which can't be owned, let alone monopolized) is the prime resource, imagination is the primary spur to development, and higher education is the key to leadership.

No society anywhere has yet converted a tight central-planning system into an economy with enough market incentive to make it dynamic, enough public-private partnership to reconcile the timidities of private investors with the rigidities of government, yet enough public regulation to ensure that corruption is contained and the disadvantaged get a fair break.

Even more than debt relief and foreign investment and technical aid, the new democracies around the world need ideas—about incentives without greed and corruption, about markets without speculation, about meeting human needs without inflation, about debt relief without austerity that beggars the poorest of the poor.

If the key question is how best to meld public planning and private enterprise, what has Canada learned that might come in handy around the world these days?

If you were to ask me the same question about U.S. experience, I would respond with a quite un-American modesty. For, come to think of it, what we also need to revive in the U.S. economy is incentives without runaway greed, markets without undue speculation, human needs met without too much inflation, debt relief without beggaring the poor. So the purpose of our relations with our newly democratic friends around the world cannot be to teach them something we know and they don't. It should be to join in a common search for what none of us has yet found—a system that combines dynamic growth with fairness.

Canada is a "Middle Power"

Canada has the capacity, in international affairs, to exercise leadership without a nuclear weapon sticking out of its back pocket. Canada is part of the natural constituency for world order, for fairness, and for protection of the Global Commons.

At important junctures in the past half-century, Canada has taken the initiative in matters of great pith and moment. A Canadian, Lester Pearson, was the first to propose a peacekeeping capability for the United Nations—and Canada has contributed many blue-helmeted soldiers-without-enemies to back up that political initiative.   Canada's development assistance and development research efforts have been among the most consistently imaginative and innovative anywhere. On China policy and arms control attitudes, Canada was well out ahead of its big southern neighbour. In economic policy, Canada recently has joined with that same neighbour in an historic pact for open trading.

Canada's strengths in information technology—computers married to electronic telecommunications—provide a natural outlet for leadership in a world where information, processed into knowledge and integrated into wisdom, is the dominant resource. There is obviously going to be a need for global systems for independent observation, inspection, and early warning to monitor both disarmament and environmental agreements.   Is there a country anywhere in a better position than Canada—because of its non-threatening size, high-tech capacity, and internationalist track record—to invent and help organize and staff them?

Canada is an Experiment in Diversity

Canada traditionally has welcomed immigrants and refugees, worried about the rights of minorities, tried to make bicultural and bilingual systems work, and generally tried to make Canada, as we must all now try to make the world, "safe for diversity."

In most countries on every continent, the settled assumption is that one race of people is permanently in charge. Only in a few exceptional cases—Canada, the United States and Brazil are the biggest ones—is there yet a public policy of assuming that any citizen has the right to seek not only freedom and fairness but political power as well. For both Canada and the United States, diversity will increasingly be our destiny, as more people from the world's congested lands seek new opportunities in the comparatively empty spaces of North America.

When Mikhail Gorbachev took the political lid off "the Communist world," what boiled over was a stewpot of diversity: almost forgotten nationalisms, everlasting ethnic and religious rivalries, external border disputes. A few of these already have surfaced—fighting on the borders of Armenia and Azerbaijan, independence in Lithuania, Latvia and Estonia, rumbles in Soviet Georgia, strikes in the Ukraine. There's much more to come. To understand the headline news of the 1990s, we're going to have to bone up on the Baltics and the Balkans, study the Soviet Union's Moslem republics, and get out our dusty atlases to find the Caucasus, the Carpathian mountains and the Crimean peninsula.

The genie of diversity is out of the bottle now, and no region of the world will escape the consequences. The idea of a multiracial, multicultural society, pioneered in fits and starts by Canada and the United States, may prove to be the great social innovation of the 1990s and beyond. Many U.S. communities already are finding, to the discomfiture of the people who got there first, that early arrival doesn't mean "majority" any more—that, as they say in Hawaii, "everybody's a minority."

So the withering of the nuclear confrontation and the flowering of fragile democracies are not, after all, the end of history. They simply reveal how very much broader, more exciting and more constructive will be our next task: to make the world safe for diversity.

Governing by Learning in an Information Society

Donald N. Michael[*]

In the beginning, so the Western legend goes, Adam and Eve ate of the tree of knowledge and, for that, they were evicted from the Garden of Eden—into, for better and worse, the Information Society. The current planetary human condition, at least that of the West, is the result of increasing amounts of information which has led to increasing creativity, and, in turn, to increasing unanticipated consequences. This state of affairs is fraught with opportunities, problems and dilemmas, which information both illuminates and complicates. Therein lie the daunting and exhilarating challenges of governing in an information society.

A fundamental consequence of increasing information, one that will cast its light—and shadow—on all that follows here, is the challenges it poses to the dominant mythologies, certainly to our Western mythology. By mythology, I mean the unquestioned beliefs shared by a society or civilization, about the purposes and ways of life that are right and natural, and that are worth maintaining. Mythologies provide a culture with its primal directions and norms.

---

[*] Donald Michael is one of the founders of research on technology assessment and on organizational and societal learning. He is Emeritus Professor of Planning and Public Policy at the University of Michigan, where he also was Program Director in the Center for Research on Utilization of Scientific Knowledge at the Institute for Social Research. He is a fellow of the American Association for the Advancement of Science, the American Psychological Association, the Society for the Psychological Study of Social Issues and the World Academy of Art and Science. He is also a member of the Club of Rome. Amongst the many books and articles he has authored are *The Unprepared Society: Planning for a Precarious Future*, and the seminal *On Learning to Plan and Planning to Learn: The Social Psychology of Changing Toward Future-Responsive Societal Learning*.

Myth lies at the basis of human society. That is because myths are general statements about the world and its parts, and in particular about nations and other in-groups, that are believed to be true and then acted upon whenever circumstances suggest or require common response. This is mankind's substitute for instinct. It is the unique and characteristic way of acting together. A people without a full quiver of relevant agreed-upon statements, accepted in advance through education or less formalized acculturation, soon finds itself in deep trouble, for, in the absence of believable myths, coherent public action becomes very difficult to improvise and sustain.[1]

Mythologies are social constructions (mostly unconscious) of reality. In the West our mythology, certainly since the Renaissance, has included beliefs that take as natural and right: individualism, science, technology, efficiency, free speech, democracy, progress, competition, a "christian" god, moral superiority, technological know-how, and male dominance. The modes of governing and the expectancies held by constituencies derive from the prevailing mythology.

These myth-engendered modes and expectancies are expressed and maintained, by boundaries—physical, ideological, factual, procedural, organizational, and relational. But these boundaries are being challenged, are disappearing, and are shifting. As a result, the processes and purposes of governing are compounded and confounded. What were outside the boundaries of organizations—externalities— have become internalities; e.g., environmental protection and child care for working parents. What were defined as internal to an organization have become matters drawing external attention; e.g., workplace safety, and the targets of "whistle blowing." All this because information, especially in an open society, encourages a situation where the conventional mythology, and the conventional boundaries that sustained and were sustained by that mythology, are under attack from many contending sources. Under attack both because, circumstances for some have not matched myth-engendered expectations (e.g., closing the rich-poor gap) and because, for others,

---

[1]"The Care and Repair of Public Myth," McNeill, W., *Foreign Affairs*, 1982, 61,1. (Thanks to Ian Stewart for introducing me to this question.)

those myth-engendered expectations are deemed undesirable (e.g., that "it's a man's world").

In recent history, especially since the Enlightenment, there has always been a tension between the conserving and the radical functions of education; that is, between learning the "answers" that provide the guidance for maintaining the society and learning to question received "wisdom;" hence, to change society. For a variety of reasons but, especially because the hardware and software of the information society have made it much easier for like interests to aggregate and for relevant information to be widely accessible, the inclination to question and the techniques for questioning—protests, tracts, data, investigative reporting, leaks, monitoring organizations, monitoring technologies, judicial injunctions, etc.—have become evermore widespread within and across societies.

Let me be clear here: I am not arguing that the traditional Western mythology and its accompanying ways of being and doing have disappeared or are about to. Quite the contrary. But I am arguing that because of its strengths and weaknesses, as perceived by "questioners" and challengers, it is becoming only one attractive, or undesirable, mythology among many. Since other myths elicit different goals and norms that may contradict or conflict with the injunctions of the traditional myth, the developing situation presents those who would govern with an ever increasing set of complexities and challenges to their authority. And this developing situation is, signally, the consequence of the proliferation of information technologies and their symbolic output.

The upshot is that governments—societies—must *learn* how to live, in as yet unformulated ways, with the complexity and turbulence engendered by evermore information. We, here and everywhere in the world, will need to alter and extend the modes and purposes of governing. We must learn as yet unformulated ways of governing because everywhere the prevailing conditions will be turbulence, uncertainty, boundary change, complexity, information overload, and feedback mal-timing. Unavoidably, reactions to those conditions will include frustration, violence, anxiety, despair, withdrawal, innovation, hope, and vision. And all of these will feed upon each other, less and less shaped and filtered by reliable boundaries and accepted myths.

But is this really a new situation? I believe it is. Generally speaking, before the emergence of the information society, actions by governments and private organizations were less pervasive, less reported upon, and less rapid in impact. Feedback regarding actions (or inactions) was slower, less sophisticated, or absent. And there were fewer actors in the governance process, and they were less well organized, less aware, and less reported about. Add to this contending myths and shifting boundaries and the context for governing becomes fundamentally different from that for which current modes and norms of governing were designed. I believe the situation is so fundamentally changed, and the consequences are so profound that the practical and ethical approach to governing ourselves in this new environment requires that we undertake the great risks and effort involved in becoming learners, as individuals and as institutions.

The task is so difficult and risky that if I believed the current modes of governing could be made adequate for what appear to be the lineaments of the information society, I would not council even trying. But I see no alternative. We must seek, somehow, to engender a persuasive mythology, wherein people believe it to be natural, desirable and possible for humans to be perpetual learners as individuals, groups and organizations, and to believe that government is rightly and naturally a prime vehicle for empowering learning.

According to such a mythology, government naturally would conduct itself as a learning system, leading the way, so to speak. In the West, at least, many still do value highly (but not unwaveringly) the spirit of exploration, research and experiment, and the quest for knowledge, the marketplace of ideas, risk-taking—all attributes of our traditional, prevailing mythic system. So, some inclinations toward norms of learning are already available. Of course, there are many cultures elsewhere and there are subcultures in the West, that do not value these standards. Living humanely with such a contending mixture of cultures is one of the challenges we must learn how to meet. I do not know how such a myth might, in fact, become the prevailing one, but I can suggest some of its necessary (but not sufficient) characteristics.

To begin with, policy and management would seek *resilience* rather than control. The idea of control, and the expectation by constituents that a competent government should be able to contrive policies that could control the ways of society, derives from the old mythology. In that mythology effect is believed to be directly and linearly related to cause, and both cause and effect are thought to be discernable through common sense or specialized competence. Knowledge of causes implied the capability to control effects. But we now live in a world so full of information that we know there are always multiple causes—indeed, more than we know about—and we know that we only know about some of the effects. In our world, control is not possible, but resilience is. Matters can be adjusted, contained within not too closely drawn boundaries, though not permanently. Therefore, learning must be unceasing. Learning is the way to resilience: resilience makes learning possible.

Becoming self-conscious learners, and learning *how* to become so, depends upon the availability of new competences in leadership, management, and in the stakeholder public. Learning happens in unique, historical contexts, especially in these turbulent times. The learning experiences of other organizations can be informative, but not definitive. Each individual, organization and society must, learn in essential ways, how to learn on its own. Risk-taking and vulnerability are, therefore, unavoidable concomitants of the learning mode. How much so will be evident as we examine other attributes of the new competency.

Uncertainty is the hallmark of the information society. Living with and *acknowledging high levels of uncertainty* is an essential attribute of the competency required for governing and being governed in an information society. While this is not the case as often in the natural sciences, in the human condition more information generally leads to more uncertainty. Usually more information tells us that we need still more information to understand a given issue, whether it be toxic substances, economic futures, welfare policy or the greenhouse effect. More information generally encourages doubts about the reliability or disinterestedness of the sources of the information. And more information provides an ever larger pool out of which interested parties can fish contending definitions of what is happening and what needs to be done. More information often stimulates the creation of more options—about which more information is needed.

Ironically, according to the old mythology, more information is expected to make decision-making easier and more decisive, but usually just the opposite happens! Living constructively and productively with uncertainty means that we shall need to discover and apply new myths, values and boundaries that define the norms and processes of government, rather than just adding more information.

Acknowledging uncertainty becomes necessary in order to highlight what still needs to be learned and, as a consequence, which activities should be monitored in order to reveal the results of policies, decisions and actions. Acknowledging uncertainty becomes a precondition for learning where we are, where we want to go, if we are getting there, and do we still want to get there.

The explicit specification of uncertainty—what we know we do not know—becomes the basis for *embracing error*, which is another attribute of the competence required for governing in an information society. Learning is the result of recognizing and using the difference between what is expected and what happens; i.e., error. Learning systems are cybernetic systems. Cybernetic systems learn from "error" information provided by feedback from the environment to which policies are directed. So, instead of hiding errors or blaming others (a basic competency in conventional governments and other organizations), in an information society competent government needs to design error-detecting systems, sensitized to acknowledged sources of uncertainty. Such systems need to reach out—to embrace—errors in order to evaluate and adjust policy and action. In other words, competent government in a turbulent,uncertain, information society must expect to make errors. Therefore, it must operate according to norms and procedures that make the most of the learning opportunities errors provide.

We shall have to learn how to design such error-embracing systems as well as how to use skillfully the information they provide. Useful feedback in cybernetic systems depends on the interplay among: the amount of information feedback; the rate at which it flows through the system; the guidance precision the feedback is intended to provide; and the match between the feedback return rate and the response rate of the system it is intended to adjust. In the nature of cybernetic systems, trade-offs are unavoidable between the information flow rates, speed of response, precision, and stability.

Currently, complex social systems manage these variables poorly and seldom recognize the ethical and operational trade-offs among them. A nice illustration of the reciprocal relationships among these variables is the conventional arguments over the procedures imposed on reporting the Middle East war. In order to reduce the potential destabilizing consequences of rapid and extensive information feedback from correspondents (made possible by the availability of new information technologies), governments reduced the precision of the information and slowed its feedback by restricting reporters' field access and censoring reports.

Early on, I emphasized that boundaries are a fundamental means by which we establish and operate our social constructions of reality, our mythic systems. In an information society, the *ability to span boundaries* appropriately is another key attribute of the new competence. Conventional competence was rewarded if it enhanced the ability of a sub-unit to protect its information and use it in its own interests, rather than those of the total system. But such sub-optimization invariably obstructs and undermines effective overall performance. Information technologies have, among their virtues, unlimited potential to span boundaries. To make full use of their capabilities requires judicious application of that spanning ability. But critical questions about the ethical and operational costs and benefits of spanning boundaries in an information society are only beginning to be recognized. For example, protecting private information versus revealing that information in order to protect the public interest (the controversy over who should have access to HIV information is a good case in point). Designing boundaries and cross-boundary flows, will require much thought and experiment, much learning of what and how.

At least as challenging as discovering appropriate modes of spanning boundaries within government is learning what ways are appropriate for spanning to the multiple and contending outside stakeholders that government must engage. Spanning across jargon, goals, operating styles and norms is difficult enough within government. Doing so successfully with external stakeholders is all the more so. Stakeholders, abetted by information and information technology, impose increasing and crosscutting demands on government and, at the same time, withdraw their trust in the competence, and even the legitimacy, of government. Ever more fragmented values and claims for rights confront government. Of course, those within government have *their* values and perspectives, shaped by their definitions of relevance, tasks and responsibilities. Those differences in values and perspectives are subject to multiple interpretations by all the involved parties. So the circle goes around again, mostly viciously, because the feedback, whether from government to stakeholders or vice versa, is usually inadequate in every respect.

Consequently, consensus becomes evermore elusive as boundaries shift, disappear and coalesce. Consensus depends on a *shared* social reality, including agreement on the legitimate means for choosing and attaining goals. Conflicts over goals, and the means for reaching them, may be reconciled if there are shared norms that can provide the basis for consensus—what Max Weber described as "the non-contractual part of the contract." But those norms, while by no means obliterated, now must contend with other norms that are made salient, and that sometimes are created through the enormous flow of ideas and data in the information society. The challenge lies in both reconciling "data bases," so to speak, and managing conflicts among differing "rules of the game," as defined by different constructions of social reality. The task for government, then, becomes not the attainment of consensus—though this is worthwhile when possible—but, realistically, the bounding and guiding of multiple consensi.

For the kind of world described here, governing translates into support for *self-conscious societal learning*. That is, stakeholders need to be centrally and deliberately involved in exposing uncertainties, creating capabilities to embrace error and, thereby, sharing with government the risks of error and the rewards of success. But, to do this, stakeholders must be sophisticated about the complexity of the issues and the concomitant costs and benefits of choices. Government, then, becomes the nexus of specialized, knowledgeable resources that can be applied to support the *joint* creation of social policy and action. Rather than pretending to provide ready-made solutions to stakeholder demands, government needs to be seen to be a powerful aid to stakeholders in the joint exploration of possible choices and, subsequently, in facilitating the implementation of those choices.

Such a learning approach is, in effect, societal research and development. To pretend that government can do more than this is to succumb to, or cynically to exploit, the old myth of controllability. The accumulated experience with citizen participation provides a good initial basis for assessing how very much more there is to learn about how and what to do in this realm of boundary-spanning in an information society.

Whatever other boundaries must be taken into account, the ability to span time boundaries is of singular importance. This must include attention to future contexts that span well beyond the preoccupations of typical political incumbents and those of most stakeholders. Among other advantages, such *future responsiveness* is an invaluable source of specifiable uncertainties (perhaps most usefully generated through multiple scenarios) that point to new options, problems and opportunities. Such a competence for extending awareness beyond the usual time horizon is necessary in order to reveal the uncertainties for which appropriate error-embracing feedback must be designed, feedback that enhances resilience and learning.

Of course, crucial to all of this are the roles of the media. Their influences on social reality—reinforcing it, obscuring it, shaping it, constructing it—are too well known to merit review here. However, I do want to underline one aspect of boundary-spanning by the media in order to emphasize another competence necessary for governing in an information society.

Public servants need to become competent as *educators* regarding both the challenges to be met and the ways to think about those challenges. Conventionally, governments make their case via presentations and public relations activities, including activities that are focused on the media. "Hearings" encourage stakeholders to make their case, and so on. All of this is necessary but, in an era of multiple myths and ever-proliferating information, this is not enough. To be an educator means to help others to learn as well as to further one's own learning. Under these circumstances, the role of the educator involves deliberately introducing new metaphors that can encourage the reperception of social reality in ways more useful for engaging this information-overloaded world. It also includes encouraging a mythology that asserts that being learners, as individuals, as organizations, and as governments—is the natural condition of humans and a prerequisite for human fulfilment.

Consider the protean function of metaphors. Metaphors are devices for setting concept and belief boundaries; tacitly they encourage expectancies and establish relationships. They reinforce social constructions of reality.

> . . . metaphor is pervasive in everyday life, not just in language but in thought and action. Our ordinary conceptual system, in terms of which we both think and act, is fundamentally metaphorical in nature.[2]

Changing the dominant metaphors, then, could be a powerful means for encouraging the reperception of the nature of problems and opportunities, for educating self and others.

In the so far dominant Western construction of reality, war-time has been a pervasive metaphor for describing peace-time activities and goals: target audiences, victorious political allies, defeating the opponents' proposals, attacking and destroying the causes of the problem. Note that sport, the other popular source of metaphors for describing civil society, depends as well on war metaphors. These metaphors tacitly emphasize we/they, before/after, winner/loser, beginning/ending, fixed boundaries in time and space and relationships that map poorly onto the amorphous information world. They encourage

---

[2] *Metaphors We Live By*, Lakolff, G. and Johnson, M., University of Chicago Press, Chicago, 1980.

the maintenance of boundaries that contribute to our inadequate responses to the problems and opportunities of an information society. But it is usually by these metaphors—data never stand alone—that governments present their policies and actions to the public, mostly through the media. They do so partially because their spokespersons also have been educated in this war/sport terminology and, therefore, think and voice their thoughts in its terms. Most importantly, they wish to talk the language of the media, whose members also think in these terms and who know that their audiences do too. Therefore, much of what the media convey maintains beliefs that are based on boundaries metaphorically reinforced by a now inadequate construction of social reality.

A mythology that emphasizes learning requires metaphors that are compatible with the purposes and experiences of learning in a fluid, amorphous world. Public servants possess extraordinarily potent leverage for precipitating change in choice of metaphor and, consequently, in how the world is perceived and attended to. Public servants are an essential information source for both the specialized and mass media. The words public servants use to inform the media can, by their choice of metaphors, educate the media. That is, persistently used, new metaphors can help media reporters, analysts, etc. to reperceive the nature and implications of the information they seek. The media, in turn, can inform their audiences in these alternative metaphoric terms and, presently, feedback to the government will begin to be expressed and, therefore, thought about, in the new metaphors, and so on around. In this way, inside government and out, changes in the metaphors that modulate the asking and answering of questions could lead toward more effective governing in an information society.

What metaphors? Ones that map a fluid, amorphous, problematic, information-rich world of multiple myths such as: reciprocity, resilience, circularity, emergence, birthing, dying, development, balance, mirroring, ebb and flow, cultivation, seeding, harvesting, potential, fittingness, both/and, multiple causality, and multiple consequences.

Less abstractly, there are metaphoric potentials to be derived from the domain of biological growth and development:

- things take time, nurturing, maturing;
- here is growth, fulfilment, decline, death;
- the unpredictable and the unique always accompany the expectable and reliable patterns of emergence from seed to bud, to bloom, to fruit, to decay, to seed.

There also are metaphoric potentials from the realm of ecology with its concepts of interdependence—"you can't do just one thing"—diversity, resilience, competition *and* collaboration, carrying capacity, vulnerability, cyclicity, continuity and, again, time for development.

There is the mirror metaphor emphasizing modeling, witnessing, facing-up-to. What does one see when the individual organization or society looks in the mirror of poverty? What does an organization mirror to its stakeholders? The broken mirror/organization splinters its reflection of reality. The distorting mirror.

There are metaphoric potentials in music. Not contradiction, but counterpoint. Dissonance, harmony, *mixed* voices and instruments. Themes and variations.

And, embracing all of these, are the learning-related metaphors: discovery, exploration, adventure, questing, knowledge, insight, new experience, risk, vulnerability, error, success.

Such metaphors could be applied to defining, explaining, legitimating, inspiring and inviting participation in governing activities in an information society. Indeed, just because information comes in so many guises, more than the current inadequate, habitual verbal and visual metaphors are necessary to reveal its meaning and import for actions and reactions to policies and programs.

We feel we understand when metaphors convey familiar meaning. And we may well understand. But the metaphors may be misleading and our understanding may be deceptive. We must learn what new metaphors better illuminate or resonate, and learn how to fine-tune them if there is to be resilient and responsive governing in an information society. The metaphoric domains mentioned here encourage and support the learning mode. Thereby, they could encourage the seeding, development and fruition of a mythic system that defines the human condition as naturally and necessarily one of individual, organizational and societal learning, and that points to government as a crucial exemplar and facilitator of learning throughout society.

There remains one more function of the public servant as educator: educating co-workers, so that they can be competent in a learning organization that, by its very nature, includes its stakeholders in the learning process. This means arranging for the education of all concerned (including oneself) in the interpersonal skills necessary to acknowledge uncertainty, embrace errors and span boundaries. Briefly, these skills involve: listening carefully; being patient with another's efforts to express a hunch or half-formed idea; being alert to, and respectful of, values other than those one espouses; being aware of the dynamics that operate within groups that, if not dealt with, obstruct the group's functioning. These, and associated skills, are critical for constructively coping with the burdens of information overload, conflicting myths, shifting boundaries and pervasive uncertainty that are ineluctably the terrain of government in an information society.[3]

Learning our way into the information society, and learning how to govern it, is necessary, risky, threatening and exhilarating. It requires that individuals, organizations and institutions be vulnerable. In exchange, learning offers the opportunity to explore and implement new definitions of social reality and, thereby, to create new possibilities for human development facilitated by felicitous modes of government. Most importantly, learning also highlights and legitimates an essential human quality, too often lost: compassion toward self as well as toward others. For, in this world, overloaded with new information and old answers, every one is in the same very leaky boat and the waves are rising.[*]

---

[3]I have explored in greater depth the rationale for a learning society, including these competences and others, in *On Learning to Plan and Planning to Learn*, Michael, Donald N., Jossey-Bass Inc., San Francisco, 1973.

[*]I am indebted to Steven Rosell, Director of the *Governing in an Information Society* project for reviewing a draft of this paper and for valuable editorial suggestions. Of course, I am soley responsible for what I have done with them.

Consensus-building and Economics

Steven A. Waldhorn[*]

Overview

This paper focuses on a set of interrelated economic challenges that modern governments face as they attempt to build more consensus among their citizens about public issues. The global economy has changed radically in the past 25 years, yet many nations are ill-equipped to deal with governance issues relating to the *new economics*. Three trends are especially important:

- First, the nature of comparative advantage has changed. Land, location, and natural resources are less important than they used to be. In countries like Canada, overall competitiveness now depends on factors such as access to technology, the skill and adaptability of the workforce, and the availability of capital.
- Second, there has been a diminution in the importance of national economies as global competition has become more significant, especially in continental economies such as the U.S.A., Canada and Russia. Regional variations are more important than ever.
- Third, the factors that produce competitiveness have changed.

---

[*] Steven A. Waldhorn is Director of the Center for Economic Competitiveness (CEC) at SRI International. CEC carries out studies in economics, technology development, human resources, and other areas related to competitiveness in today's global economy. In recent years, Mr. Waldhorn has overseen studies for national governments in the United States, Canada, France, and China; for business leadership groups in Hong Kong, Spain, and in a number of U.S. states; for state governors in Minnesota, Florida, Michigan, and California; for regional governments in Australia, China, Malaysia, India and Germany, as well as for international organizations. He currently is involved in regional economic strategy development in Czechoslovakia and Yugoslavia. He has authored, or co-authored, more than 20 articles and books on economic development and public planning.

Today a new role is being played by "agglomeration economies"—the role Hong Kong plays in garments, Silicon Valley in computers, New York in finance, and Nogoya in automotives—which develop new product lines, set prices, and establish worldwide distribution channels for their products. As a consequence, they capture the largest share of the value-added international trade in their product areas. Serving only as a site for branch plants or as a source for raw materials is a less and less rewarding economic role for a country to play.

The New Economics

Comparative advantage today is dependent on two new sets of factors: the presence, or lack, of sound economic infrastructure and the existence of concentrations, or "clusters," of industry. At SRI we have worked on developing clusters and infrastructure in the U.S. and Canada; around the Pacific Rim—from India to Australia; in Western Europe; and in formerly socialist countries in Central Europe and the former U.S.S.R.

Because of these factors, in the past decade some regions have prospered in the global economy, while others in the same nation have fared poorly. In the U.S., for instance, Department of Commerce figures confirm that 1980 saw the end of *50 years* of U.S.A. regions' per capita income converging. Since then, each of our regions has begun to go its own way; some down and then up, like the Great Lakes, some up and then down, like the Northeast.

Around the world, similar disparities occur. In the United Kingdom, between London and Northern England; in Japan, between Tokyo and outlying prefectures; in China, between the south and the centre and the north; and in Canada, between Ontario and the remainder of the Confederation. In each case, areas prospering have the requisite clusters of industry and economic infrastructure that modern economies need.

The difference that clusters of industries and economic infrastructure can make in an economy is well illustrated by the example of southern China. In the past decade, thousands of factories have been established, in Quandong, next to Hong Kong. They produce toys, garments and sophisticated electronics. Hong Kong, which is linked to Quandong by a light railway, has supplied the economic resources to make Quandong's industry productive: workers are trained by professionals from Hong Kong; Hong Kong banks provide money for equipment; Hong Kong managers live for short stints in dwellings supplied by the factory (and return home for weekends). Because Hong Kong's economic infrastructure has been available to southern China, the five per cent of China's population who are in the area adjacent to Hong Kong now produce over 30 per cent of the country's foreign exchange earnings and southern China's Special Economic Zones (SEZ) have been extraordinarily successful. One, Szenchen, has grown from 80,000 to 1.5 million people in eight years. At the same time, SEZs in northern and central China have been unsuccessful.

Thus Hong Kong also illustrates the second factor in the new economics. Once the macroeconomic requisites for growth have been put into place, economic policy becomes largely regional policy. Differences in industrial structure and economic infrastructure drive different regions in the same country in different directions, in response to changing world demand. Today, events in Tokyo often have more influence on California, and events in the Middle East have more influence on the U.S. energy belt than many actions taken in Washington, D.C. This regionalization of economics is, of course, not irrelevant to recent developments in Ottawa. Every country needs to find ways to regionalize economic planning.

This brings us to the third factor: the new importance of economic clusters. Today, geographic concentrations of producers and suppliers linked together through complex webs of buyer/supplier linkages are what fuel innovation in many industries. Value added in internationally traded manufactured goods is derived less and less from the process of manufacturing (inasmuch as many goods can be "pasted together" almost anywhere in the world), but arises from sourcing, research and development (R&D), and distribution. And sourcing, R&D and distribution require concentrations of industry.

Suppose an entrepreneur wants to develop a new computer peripheral. If he is in San Jose, California, it is not difficult to find someone who can provide the right microchip, another person who can provide software, and a third who can get it "on the shelves" at retail outlets. This local concentration of talent resulted in a centre of geographic innovation–Silicon Valley–which, in turn, is utilized by international companies that develop and market innovations worldwide.

Or, suppose an international company wants to develop a new line of clothes. In Hong Kong, it can easily find designers, material suppliers, contractors who can get goods cut and sewn in China or Brazil, and brokers who can provide assistance regarding American and European quotas. This local concentration of talent, in turn, fuels international trade in consumer-oriented industries such as clothing.

On the other hand, if a company tries to develop a new piece of computer equipment or a new line of clothes in an isolated location, it might never put all of the pieces together. The relevant question is: can governments purposefully help create centres of agglom-eration or link sub-regions to such centres through policy?

Consensus-building and the New Economics

Consensus-building is much to the point here. Over the past two decades Japan and the newly industrialized economies (NIEs) have shown how economic infrastructure can be built. Such market-oriented economic planning is as much an exercise in political consensus-building as it is an economic endeavour. Developing new agglom-erations of industry to produce world-class products can only be accomplished through the use of decision-making processes that involve consensus-type approaches. Thus, a key question for govern-ment at the end of the 20th century is how to build such consensus; in other words how to move the political dialogue in this direction.

Some SRI projects show how one can develop consensus on economic issues. This work—which extends worldwide—involves helping public and private leaders to analyse issues and decide how to move ahead on a common agenda. There is an international dialogue taking place about how economic regions should organize themselves. The common elements of this dialogue—which revolve around how to build consensus on economic directions—are in many ways more important than the differences found in diverse economies around the world.

The American Midwest

One good example is provided by the American Midwest, the industrial Midwest, which in the early 1980s had to face twin recessions, buffeted by international competition. It is now clear that, essentially, what was happening was the end of mass production and the old industrial economy and the beginning of the post-industrial economy, characterized by a lot more information content in goods, a lot more flexibility and adaptability, much shorter periods of design and so on—a revolution in production. The region was very ill-prepared to deal with this fundamental change; there was widespread demoralization; people were emigrating; there was no consensus about what needed to be done. There was a lot of talk about particular issues; e.g., that labour unions were a major bar to productivity, but every part of the community had problems. The universities took narrow academic perspectives and didn't work closely with industry; financial laws in most of the states were obsolete; and public training programs were ineffective. In short, all of the institutions that were central to a new economic infrastructure (the universities, training programs, state agencies, unions and businesses) were looking after themselves and had no common vision of where the region should go. Traditional economists were forecasting that the decline was bound to continue.

In this environment, a number of people, including both Republican and Democratic governors and a number of private groups, started saying that it was time to create a new vision that people could believe in. A series of analytic reports were commissioned that tried to lay out how to re-invigorate the manufacturing sector and what the institutions of the Midwest would need to do if the economy was to prosper.[1] Public-private task forces were created. There was an immense, and increasingly co-operative effort to look at the roles of government and business and to expand their roles to cover a wider conception of economic infrastructure.

The results were striking. In recent years, the Midwest has led the U.S. economy, and is now leading the country out of the recession. The array of organizations involved have become more sensitized to their common interests; e.g., pension fund administrators now accept a small additional risk in order to finance local industry.

The process through which this happened involved analytic activity—definition of a vision of a slimmed down, technologically improved, more highly trained economy; continuous work over many months and, in some cases years, by public and private task forces; the publication of many reports; and heavy involvement of the media. Elected leaders also encouraged efforts. For example, President Reagan, at the same time that he was shedding federal responsibilities for regional development in the U.S.A., made a special trip to the Midwest to encourage people to work on these issues. As a result, the region came to understand that it was under-investing in itself and that there was a need to increase such investment and, based on that consensus, taxes were raised, new programs were implemented, and the results have been very encouraging.

---

[1]*Choosing a Future: Steps to Revitalize the MidAmerican Economy Over the Next Decade*, SRI, 1984.
Investing in the Future: A Prospectus for MidAmerica, SRI, 1986.
Indicators of Economic Capacity, SRI, 1986.

Baltimore, Maryland

A second example of how to build consensus is provided by Baltimore, Maryland. The Baltimore area has a bifurcated economy, with major, federal R&D laboratories on the one hand and a traditional manufacturing sector on the other. Johns Hopkins University views itself as a world university, not connected to the local economy, and so, in general, there is very little connection between the world of research and that of business. A working coalition of Chief Executive Officers (CEOs) from both public and private institutions came to see this as a real issue for the future economic development of the region, and energized a group called the Greater Baltimore Committee. The committee commissioned a report that laid out an agenda for a new business school in Baltimore, provided a design for new apprenticeship training programs for the community, and suggested linking Johns Hopkins more closely to the R&D needs of Maryland.[2]

Because business, government, and university leaders were involved, the report was greeted with great excitement. Two million dollars was raised from private sources for implementation. That two million dollars was leveraged into a 200 million dollar program supported by the Governor to modernize the science and technology infrastructure of Maryland. And that 200 million dollar program is having a major effect on the two billion dollars worth of federal spending in the federal laboratories located in the state. So, a small $150,000 exercise can have tremendous potency. And, as an additional benefit, the business community came out of the effort understanding their responsibilities towards the institutions on whose boards they sit, and a real working consensus was created amongst educators, scientists, government people, business persons and other elements in the community. A public/private-sector coalition was key to making this happen, as has been the case in many similar efforts in which SRI has been involved.

---

[2]*From Bystander to Leader: Challenging Higher Education to Join in Building Baltimore's Economic Future*, SRI, 1988.

Karnataka, India

In Karnataka, India's best high-technology state, there is no shortage of intellectual resources, but they are all separated by bureaucratic barriers. There are 23 engineering schools with curricula that haven't been updated since 1947. A public/private initiative in Karnataka was able to cut through the traditional bureaucratic divisions by showing both business leaders and academicians what was at stake and how, by working together, they could make Karnataka be more competitive internationally.[3] Again, public/private task forces were key in generating a broad vision to which all could subscribe and then, because of India's poverty, international aid programs from Germany, Sweden, and the U.S.A. contributed funds to help realize the vision. Those public/private task forces continue in operation today because the private sector understands how much they have to gain by working with public institutions, and the public sector understands that developing human resources, technology and financial strategies must be a public/private effort.

Hong Kong

A fourth example is provided by Hong Kong. SRI spent five years working there on the development of an economic strategy, and during this process had to deal with a traditional separation between economic and governmental activity. On the one hand, the Chinese traditionally have had little to do with the governance of Hong Kong, while the British, on the other, traditionally have insisted that public administration has no economic impact. Their philosophy is enshrined in the so-called doctrine of "positive non-intervention." A study was done which demonstrated to both sides that Hong Kong was under-investing in comparison with its competitors in Singapore, Taiwan and other places.[4] The result was a new, local philosophy of economic partnership.

---

[3] *A Blue Print For Action*, SRI, 1988.
[4]*Building Prosperity: A Five-Part Economic Stretegy for Hong Kong's Future*, SRI,1989.

Reaching a shared awareness that a new philosophy is needed is a critical issue in all of the places in which SRI has worked: it is necessary to allow sufficient time for the members of a community, public and private, to come together.

And, this coming together is a bottom-up, not a top-down, process. One key meeting in Hong Kong was between the Financial Secretary of the government and leading members of the business community. The Financial Secretary said he represented a government constrained because it was leaving office in six years (when China will take over Hong Kong) and told the business leaders that he could only take certain actions if they "pushed" him to do so. The business leaders replied: "If you tell us what to do so, we'll push you;" but the Financial Secretary said: "No, I can't give you power, you have to take it." This is directly parallel to a famous maxim by the American community organizer Saul Alinsky, who counselled community groups in the U.S. on how to achieve power for over 20 years. While the top has to be open to a process of collaboration, other elements have to take initiatives. In other words, government leaders can't build consensus by themselves.

The Importance of Vision

One clear finding emerges from all of these studies—a vision that people can share is of critical importance. A clear example of this is provided by the state of Nebraska. Nebraska has been a corn economy, but for the last 14 years Nebraska has not made any net income from corn, aside from federal benefits. Nebraska's small towns are being depopulated, but the idea of Nebraska as a corn economy is an icon in the state legislature. Yet, it proved possible to move the dialogue toward developing an alternate vision of what the state could be by doing an analysis of the changing role of agriculture; by getting newspapers to give the analysis publicity; by forming task forces; and by holding public meetings around Nebraska.[5]

---

[5] *New Seeds for Nebreaska: Strategies for Building the Next Economy*, SRI, 1987.

A vision sounds like something mystic, but in fact what it does is give people a logic to help them to understand themselves and their local economy in a new way. In the case of Nebraska it was understanding that it is not a corn-growing state, but the place you reach in the U.S. when somebody dials an 800 number—an information-processing state. *When you give people a new vision, they are able to develop, if a process exists, an alternate rationale for their institutions whether they be scientific or business or educational. It is this blending of analysis with process to generate a new vision, that can be so important in moving towards consensus.*

Temporary Structures

A related point that cuts across the issues is that all of the efforts described involve the creation of temporary structures in which public/private groups took on roles that previously were thought to be the domain of government. These are temporary expedients to deal with more systemic problems in the nature of governance in the current circumstances. An issue that arises, then, is how can we move from these temporary expedients to something that might be more lasting? It may be that the area at which we are more likely to be able to develop more lasting approaches is that of the economy at the regional level, which is effectively where most of the economic action now is. It is there that we need to build enduring visions and new kinds of institutions to implement them.

The Educative Role of Government

Finally, much of what this paper has described really comes down to government's educative role. It is said that the nation state is a rather fragile idea, that nations in some respects are both too small and too big to do the key jobs that need to be done. It may be the case that much of the purpose of national government is to represent the different regional agglomerations where economic competitiveness is developed today. National governments should be responsible for taking the requirements of individual regions, relate them to each other, and represent them at national and international levels. But in order for this to happen, regions need to have a notion of what they are about and what they need from national or international fora. So another role national government must play is to increase the capacity of different parts of a country to articulate visions as well as to develop the kinds of infrastructure they need to make visions happen—new kinds of infrastructure, not the canals and railroads of yesterday, but the ingredients for success today and tomorrow.

So, the question of consensus-building at the national level may come down to what role can different national ministries play in creating fora for solving particular problems relating to regional economies: how to create the infrastructure that is needed; how to decide what industries to develop; and the implications of this for regional balance, and so on. All nations need these kinds of educative, problem-solving processes.

An interesting question is: why have the Anglo Saxon democracies—such as the U.S.A., Australia and Canada—had a great deal of trouble over the last 10 or 15 years coming together to do this kind of problem-solving, relative to countries like Germany, France and Japan. How can we do better in forging consensus with respect to the kinds of fundamental issues that will shape the future prosperity of our nations and regions? These putatively "economic" questions, in fact, may be the most important political challenges our nations will face as we approach the 21st century.

Reflections on the Business of Governing in an Information Society

Peter Trueman[*]

In this last decade of the 1990s, a critical period for the Canadian confederation, it is clear that the Canadian mass media, as purveyors of essential information to voters wishing to make intelligent decisions, are at best unreliable. And even journalists who see this as a problem are able to make very few suggestions about how government might use the media more effectively in communicating with its constituency.

It isn't just that news has become what one of our best TV news producers calls "a lousy narrow structure," governed less by the ethics of journalism than by the quest for large audiences and big circulations. Those dismayed by what appears to be the unbridgeable gulf between government and the governed also seem to believe that society is foundering under a data overload that it can neither catalogue nor absorb. If there is a light at the end of the tunnel, it is the role the computer might ultimately play in eliminating the journalist as the only middleman.

There is an overwhelming variety of information from an overwhelming variety of sources. As a freelance writer and columnist, I must sift tons of the stuff, not only to stay reasonably well informed about current affairs, but to find those nuggets of information from which ideas grow and which suggest fresh approaches to old subjects.

---

[*] Peter Trueman is an award-winning author, broadcaster and reporter. He has been a correspondent with the *Montreal Star* and the *Toronto Star*. He was a writer, executive producer and, later, Head of News at the English television network of the Canadian Broadcasting Corporation. From 1973 to 1988 he was the Anchor of the Global Television Network news. He currently is a contributor to numerous publications including *Starweek Magazine* and the *Kingston Whig-Standard*.

I read three daily newspapers from front to back, and clip articles I need for my files. I read books on the subjects that interest me, two weekly news magazines, and other periodicals. I listen to a good deal of radio, both domestic and short wave, and I watch two daily TV news programs and other information programming. This takes a minimum of 30 hours a week, time I would and could not spare if my living did not depend on it.

And even then I feel hard-pressed, so I have great sympathy for the man or woman who spends from eight to 12 hours a day at a challenging job and who comes home in the evening and says: "To hell with it! What I need is a leisurely meal, a squash game, a thriller or something entertaining on TV. Not more facts and figures and hard choices. I don't want to think any more."

What harried professionals say they need most is the essential news filtered for them. In effect, they need someone reliable to make decisions about what news they ought to consume.

But the problem with that, it seems to me, is that the producers and editors who are willing to filter for a busy readership or audience, tend not to be very trustworthy. Take U*SA Today*, a publication which American anchor Linda Ellerbee once described as a newspaper for those who find TV news too complicated. *USA Today* filters the news, it's true, but it doesn't do nearly as well as *The Wall Street Journal*, for example, in explaining the business of government to those at the receiving end. And I, for one, wouldn't allow *USA Today* to do any filtering for me. Why would I trust a publication which is more interested in making its readers feel good than in serious journalism?

But all newspapers are under pressure to change because of shifting patterns of consumption, and even those which see themselves as newspapers of record have given up any idea of trying to impart a major part of that record to their readership on a daily basis. The real challenge is no longer to get the most news first and most accurately, or to increase advertising, or even to increase circulation. It is to hold the attention of existing readers say for 20 minutes a day.

The *Globe and Mail* is a newspaper for people who read, I would say. The *London Free Press*, on the other hand, which has moved down market towards *USA Today*, and which uses more pictures, shorter stories, and splashier graphics, is a newspaper for people who haven't got time to read a real one.

The *Kingston Whig-Standard*, which publishes a column of mine every week, is a newspaper produced by writers, not graphic artists. But the *Whig*, the country's oldest daily newspaper, and until recently owned by a single family, has just been bought by Southam. The previous owner said he could find no way to pass the paper on to his son without loading him down with enormous debt, and could find no way to give the paper adequate financial resources even in the short run. Southam is a responsible chain, as chains go, but I am not confident that the *Whig* will remain unchanged in the teeth of the obvious market realities.

There was an interesting piece in the *Ottawa Citizen* recently quoting Peter Murdoch, a former *Hamilton Spectator* deskman who has been organizing for the newspaper guild. He says that the union is enjoying its greatest growth in 30 years, not because news people are worried about job security, or pay and benefits, but because, as he puts it, "journalism is under attack."

Murdoch says there is "a much stronger management culture in newspapers, and the emphasis is on the bottom line." He adds that increasingly journalists feel threatened. "They believe their role in a democratic society is not just to get out and sell, but to provide information on complex issues to a frequently confused electorate," he suggests. But if good journalists still believe that people deserve more and better hard information than they are currently getting, and the population feels the same way, why hasn't there been a public outcry?

The fact of the matter is that if we once believed we had a right to information, we now seem to believe we have a right to entertainment. Leisure is sacred, and one of the hallmarks of the new North American society is impatience. Even some of us with a taste for haut cuisine, for example, find it increasingly difficult to interrupt a journey by car for a properly cooked meal, when we can grab a Big Mac and a coffee and be on our way again in five minutes. And it doesn't seem to matter whether we're working, or on vacation.

Because our appetites have changed, the new technology and the new ease of transmission is not having the desired effect. As Henry David Thoreau warned us in "Walden" a century and a half ago, advances in communications haven't necessarily been beneficial. "We are in haste to construct a magnetic telegraph from Maine to Texas," he noted, "but Maine and Texas, it may be, have nothing important to communicate."

Thoreau ridiculed the notion that speedier communication would in itself be desirable, "as if," as he put it, "the main object were to talk fast and not sensibly. We are eager to tunnel under the Atlantic and bring the Old World some weeks nearer to the new; but perhaps the first news that will leak through into the broad, flapping American ear will be that Princess Adelaide has the whooping cough."

Some of us dared to hope that the all-news networks would be the answer for serious TV journalists. But I would be a lot happier about the Cable News Network (and about Newsworld too, I suspect, although I haven't seen much of it) if their round-the-clock capabilities were used for lengthier, more intensive examination and discussion.

As it is, there is a tendency, at least on CNN, to perpetuate the awful compression of the standard TV newscast. A one minute and thirty second item, even if it is replaced by a new item of the same length each half hour, still adds up to 90 seconds of highlights. So CNN and Newsworld could be valuable, in my view, precisely to the extent that they abandon the old newscast formats and break new ground. I'm not holding my breath for them to do that, somehow.

Before television began to change the way we think, it was generally assumed by those in charge of newsrooms that the primary purpose of news was to transfer information; that the audience should be given information it needed, whether it knew it or not (or perhaps wanted it or not); that the news should be timely and deal with matters of intrinsic importance; and that there should be a descending order of magnitude in what was reported.

The most important stories were on page one, and the least important stories were back with the truss ads. Stories were written in what was called the inverted pyramid style. Who did what to whom, when, where, why, and how were the most important questions, and the answers were usually supplied in the first paragraph. Lesser facts followed in succeeding paragraphs, which meant that an editor who was short of space could cut the story from the bottom up, without losing the most important facts and quotations.

Television news, when it began, aped the newspaper. The most important news led the newscast and the least important closed it. But the dynamics of television soon began to change all that. It became apparent, for one thing, that the place of honour in a newscast was not necessarily first. What was said last was often memorable. Then too, the most important news of the day—a constitutional development, for example—might have the least interesting pictures. In television, where production considerations are often paramount, the rule is to lead with the best visuals, so as to hook the viewer and persuade him to stay around. News began to become not what was important, as the newspapers defined important, but what you had film of.

In TV news, visual literacy began to replace print literacy. A narrative style borrowed from film and theatre began to shape the structures of news stories. Facts were no longer strung together in descending order of importance, the way they were in print, but were linked dramatically, in an attempt to hold the viewer to the very end, not only to the end of the story, but to the end of the newscast. News stories, like vaudeville jokes, had begun to have punchlines. The freshness and immediacy of stories began to matter more than the light they shed on the human condition, or on the problems of daily living.

New TV networks and stations were licensed, and cable systems began to deliver an incredible choice of signals. Attracting a mass audience became increasingly difficult, and the industry's emphasis began to shift to so-called "narrowcasting." It also made conventional broadcasters, already pandering to their audiences, rely more shamelessly than ever on market research. As the "show doctors" took over, they prescribed interesting, entertaining and relevant news to replace news once labelled "important."

TV news producers began giving people the news they wanted, not the news they needed, and complex issues were either reduced to absurd generalities or bumped from the line-up completely by a new breed of non-stories on traffic, the weather, motherhood, lifestyle and the sort of thing that used to be reserved for Ripley's Believe-It-Or-Not.

"The corporate culture operating within media demands adherence to this simplification," says one senior TV news producer. "And managers tend to hire and promote its advocates. It has taken on aspects of a theology and calls itself 'democratization of information.' It tends to disguise a creeping anti-intellectualism fostered, in part, by a generation of journalists who have not needed to understand complexity because their product is invariably reduced to the sum of the simplest common elements of any issue."

Perhaps TV newscasts should have been required to carry a warning label to the effect that story placement no longer reflected the intrinsic importance of a news item. Unaware that the rules had changed, an audience that watched a newscast in which the first seven items were devoted to Ben Johnson testing positive at the Olympics, for example, might be forgiven for assuming that one sprinter taking steroids was infinitely more important than Pat Carney's resignation from the federal cabinet, covered only briefly in a short "voice over" near the end of the newscast.

What this means to those in government who worry about informing the electorate is that the mass media is less and less useful to them, and, in some ways, less and less dangerous as well. This inability to get the mass media to deal adequately or persistently with serious issues can sometimes have its advantages, at least for the bureaucracy.

The media, even the print variety, increasingly overlook stories on government which are too complex, too dull visually, too time-consuming, or dependent on facts that are too hard to pin down. Some bureaucrats and politicians have come to rely on the media's distaste for hard work and its short attention span to keep reporters away from stories that could be embarrassing.

What the media does report, of course, can have enormous impact. Concentrated and incessant reporting of major news events in the mass media can influence politicians and the formulation of public policy dramatically. One thinks of the overthrow of Marcos in the Philippines, Tiananmen Square, the tension leading up to the failure of the Meech Lake accord, the stand-off with the Mohawks at Oka, and one of the major international stories of our time, the failure of the diplomatic process in the Persian Gulf and the high tech shoot-out which followed.

In the weeks leading up to the war, was the media pushing for the worst outcome, for the sake of a story, as some people feared, or was the American military pushing the media? If we have come to expect that we should be entertained by news, do reporters give short shrift to diplomacy and, if war comes, do they cover it as if it were a football game?

Few journalists believe that the media is capable of stampeding the U.S.A. or any other country into armed conflict. As a matter of fact, since Vietnam, certainly in the eyes of the military, the media has been feared as a force more likely to ruin a good war than to promote one.

It was that point of view, certainly, that gave rise to the unprecedented information lock-out staged by the U.S.A. and other allied military during the war in the Gulf. The press took a beating. Journalists were treated harshly by governmental spokesmen and the military, who were egged on by the general public. Most North Americans seemed to think that indulging the media would inevitably result in the wholesale publication of information that would be of aid and comfort to the Iraqis.

But in my experience, few journalists have any objection to traditional military censorship, that is the excising of strategic information from copy, scripts and visuals before publication or broadcast is permitted.

What they were objecting to so strenuously during the Gulf War was that most of the censorship was taking place in advance. Reporters were forced to operate in herds, far from the front lines, and were prevented physically from using their own eyes, ears and powers of inquiry to collect the raw information from which their stories were constructed. When you limit journalists to press briefings, news releases and pool reports from a chosen few standing in for them in carefully orchestrated combat situations, you condemn them to reporting without understanding, the ultimate journalistic failing.

The public's acquiescence to this awful erosion of media capability has been alarming. In my view, what happened to reporters during the Persian Gulf crisis was as dangerous to good government as it was to responsible journalism.

What has been missing in the public assessment of recent media developments, it seems to me, is any sense that we are on the edge of yet another information breakthrough, perhaps one of even greater magnitude than the changeover from print to television.

In another decade or two, the informational emphasis may have shifted beyond recognition. As people become less willing to spend time "filtering" the news, in order to find what is interesting or important to them, it seems likely that, increasingly, they will be given the opportunity to become their own editors and producers.

The futurists and the technical experts assure us that television, for example, will soon become interactive. If the viewer is particularly interested in something that appears briefly on his screen, he'll be able to push a "show-me-more" button to explore it in greater depth. He will, to some extent, be able to produce his own program.

Similarly, people scanning the encapsulated daily news bulletins delivered to their home screens via fibre optics and personal computers will be able to scroll through items of little interest, and call up additional details on stories they believe are important to them personally and professionally. In effect, they will be able to do their own editing.

We're not talking about the distant future. Commercial systems with this interactive capability are already in place and are likely to gain impetus from the fact that the generation now in the ascendancy understands better when it's doing something, not just watching something, or reading something. Thus, a variety of interactive informational systems, available in both home and office, may be government's main link with every segment of its constituency by early in the next century.

Dr. Robert K. Logan, a University of Toronto Physics professor who is cross-appointed to the Ontario Institute of Studies in Education, where he teaches and carries out research on computer applications in the school system, collaborated with the late Marshall McLuhan. In a book called "The Alphabet Effect," Dr. Logan notes:

> The computer coupled to a printer converts every school child into a publisher and reinforces the notion of writing as a communications activity rather than a dreadful and empty school exercise. The preliminary experience with word processing has been so positive that it is likely that the computer will be the inspiration for a new burst of literary activity similar to the one that accompanied the advent of the printing press. . . .

> One possible explanation for this phenomenon, which represents a reversal of the malaise towards books and schoolwork that television inspired, . . . is that the computer is the first medium to compete successfully against TV for the child's attention.

It was the video game, cited so often during the Gulf War, that broke the ice:

> Despite initial fears regarding addiction, writes Prof. Logan, most children tire of the video game and transfer their addiction to computers, which contain many of the features about video games that they like, such as instant response or feedback, the interactivity with the system, and the ability to control the video environment.

> Rather than becoming passive consumers of video images, children are able to control the video environment, at first responding to pre-programmed games and then by creating their own images and games by programming the computer themselves.

We should perhaps make a distinction not just between information and news, but between information and knowledge. Dr. Daniel Boorstin, formerly of the U.S. Library of Congress, made the point on television recently that with information systems like CNN, in which news is recycled and broadcast every half hour, information actually displaces knowledge. Knowledge has endured, Dr. Boorstin said, because it describes the world over generations, not day by day.

When citizens, by interacting with those in charge of input for their television screens and computers, actually engage in conversation with journalists and civil servants, knowledge may finally be restored to its rightful eminence. And the market for journalistic trivia, now a mainstay of the mass media, could be expected to diminish.

New Technologies and Democratic Governance

Mary Ann Young[*]

In this paper I will outline some experiences we have had in the United States in using interactive information technology to promote public participation in government policy-making. I hope this will provide a basis for comparison with your experience here in Canada.

Many politicians and political analysts in America think that public input should be limited. The ideal politician, according to the writers of the United States Constitution, is a leader/statesman, somewhat removed from the pressures of individual citizens, who focuses on the common good. That ideal is not evident in politicians today, if ever it was, as they increasingly are forced to focus on the latest polls, where the campaign money is coming from, and which issues and 30-second spots will get them on the evening television news show.

There has been a significant increase, however, in individuals wanting to exert more control over their own lives. This is evident in civil rights movements, in increased activism in environmental and other public policy areas, in demands for more control over education by teachers and students, and in demands by individuals for more knowledge and choice in health care.

At the same time, many citizens feel that it is futile to participate in governmental policy-making. Apathy and alienation abound. There is something drastically wrong with communication between citizens and their government if the flood of "citizen discontent" stories of recent years are to be believed. From a low point in the 1930s during the Great Depression until the mid-1960s, a majority of citizens gave positive evaluations of government. Massive change occurred in the mid-1960s. Poll after poll since then has shown declining confidence in government.

[*]Mary Ann Young was a senior researcher with the United States Office of Technology Assessment (OTA) when she undertook the research which is the basis of this paper. While at OTA, Ms. Young also performed research on issues of office automation, electronic surveillance, and the effects of technological change on constitutional law. Ms. Young also has undertaken and directed research projects at the Institute for Workplace Learning and at the McDonnell Douglas Corporation.

Why Should We Care?

Voters lack enough information to make good choices and voting does not give good information to the governors either. They do not really know why they were elected—was it charisma, taxes, the economy, more governmental regulation, less governmental regulation? A recent newspaper story illustrates the ineptness of many analysts.

> He [the child] broke the green lamp, which means either that he thinks we keep the place too bright or else that he hates green. Do we buy smaller bulbs or a different coloured lamp?
>
> Neither. You'll notice he threw the lamp through the window. Obviously he senses a need for fresh air.
>
> Of course! And what are we to make of the fact that he blamed the whole thing on the dog?[1]

Why should we care that many people do not participate? Because democracy cannot survive without the participation of most of the citizens. Political leaders will become increasingly distanced from the needs of the people and will, thus, make more "mistakes" in developing programs and regulations. The resulting distrust on the part of the public will make the consensus necessary for dealing with today's complex and far-reaching problems difficult, if not impossible.

Such alienation also allows the rise of extremist ideologies such as occurred in the 1991 election for Governor of the State of Louisiana. The government has become so far removed from the needs of the people that 40 per cent of Louisiana citizens voted for David Duke, a former head of the Ku Klux Klan and a professed admirer of Hitler. We can only hope that most of those who voted for him were not truly admiring Duke, but were trying to loudly and clearly get the government's attention on issues of concern to them.

---

[1]Raspberry, William, "Decoding the Tantrum Vote," *Washington Post* , November 11, 1991, p. A19.

The messenger may be different next time, but the message will remain the same. These kinds of extremist ideologies have always been around in a very small minority of United States citizens, but have been kept under control. That control could disappear if widespread citizen participation in policy-making is not promoted and achieved.

The quality of life in any society also deteriorates as more people become more alienated from their government. Divisions between groups of people become more intense. Crime increases as the number of people excluded from the system becomes larger and more entrenched.

How Can Participation Be Increased?

Should participation be encouraged even for those who don't understand the issues? More information and more discussion of public policy issues will lead to more understanding and more consensus on objectives and values to be pursued. The more discussion takes place, the less likely are politicians to be surprised with revolts and loss of their positions, and citizens will be better able to forestall expensive and destructive political activities. For example, Lech Walesa has said that information dispensed through computers and satellite TV would make it impossible for a Stalin to murder people today.[2]

New telecommunications technologies, although not necessary for communication between governors and their constituents, can help in providing more and better information. Besides aiding in more effective delivery of government services, communication networks can allow more people to become involved in public policy discussions. As this occurs, governors will have little choice about whether or not to become involved themselves or about who will participate.

---

[2]Rosenstiel, Thomas B., "TV, VCRs Fan Fire of Revolution: Technology Served the Cause of Liberation in East Europe. The Power of Information is Clear, But is it Democratizing?", *Los Angeles Times*, January 18, 1990, p. A1.

If political leaders think of their role as managing and mediating the process of governance, they can use new technologies to deal with the larger inflow of information that is occurring and to mediate a process that already is taking place. The task of governors will be to filter discussion and proposed solutions in order to eliminate the radical and irrelevant and to steer discussions toward workable decisions. In addition to providing broader and deeper public input to policy-making, computers can analyze information received in a way not previously possible, aiding in the search for viable solutions to problems.

Providing Government Information

There are numerous current examples of telecommunications technologies being used by city, county and state governments in the U.S.A. to govern more efficiently and effectively. These technologies are being used to manage governmental information and to administer governmental services, and they can be used more extensively to promote public policy discussion in the future. By the end of the decade, approximately 80 per cent of all governmental information will be automated.[3] Computers can provide information 24 hours per day, relieve governmental employees of burdensome information-providing tasks, and eliminate the need to cut services when finances contract.

The most common use of telecommunications technologies is to provide governmental information. The 24-Hour City Hall[4] is a concept that has been promoted for only a couple of years, but is

---

[3]McCarty, Kathryn Shane, "Electronic Democracy," *Special Report: Technology Now Allows 24-Hour Access to Information*, National League of Cities, September 9, 1991.

[4] The 24-Hour City Hall is a trademarked service made available through a public/private partnership between Public Technology, Inc. (a research, development and commercialization arm of the National League of Cities, the National Association of Counties and the International City/County Management Association) and the IBM Corporation.

spreading rapidly among local governments. The 24-Hour City Hall uses a touchscreen computer with text and graphics to inform the public about available governmental services. The computer screens are placed in shopping malls and other easily accessed locations. The systems not only provide citizens with fast, accurate information about their government and community, but improve the knowledge of the public about governmental services. The governments benefit from the systems in that fewer personnel and less time need be devoted to providing information in response to phone calls. The result is less cost to government, less frustration and more information for the public, and a more positive image of government in the public mind. Some communities that have installed 24-Hour City Halls include:

Kansas City, Missouri—City Hall in the Mall—logged 50,000 calls last year on a budget of $268,435; installed in shopping malls; covers neighbourhood organization activity, governmental representatives at local, state and national levels, an Action Centre data bank, city council agendas, upcoming events and the schedule of the government access cable TV channel.

Hillsborough County, Florida—The 24-Hour Courthouse—logged 400,000 calls last year on a budget of $380,000; lists general county information, job listings and application procedures, legislative issues, recent bids and awards, and information on local, state and national governmental representatives; installed in shopping malls and libraries (one is a mobile unit).

Mercer Island, Washington—Island Epicenter—a co-operative venture with a local grocery store that is open 24 hours a day; the store contributed hardware, software and space; offers over 100 files of city information, including how to obtain licenses and permits, city council meeting schedules and recreational programs.

Providing Governmental Services

The next step is to provide actual services via computers—accept applications for various licenses, accept tax forms and business form filings, and provide government-collected data online. Some communities are beginning to provide these online services. The cost of providing these services online is preventing many governments who are strapped financially now from doing so. Some charge fees for services provided in order to overcome the financial restraints. Prince Georges County, Maryland recently has begun providing court docket information online for a fee to lawyers. They plan to expand this service to property assessment data in the near future. By providing services now that can pay their own way, they hope to pave the way for free services to the public later on.

Santa Monica, California accepts applications for business licenses and permits online, and also allows people to sign up for recreational facilities, renew and order library items, and file consumer complaints and petty theft forms.

Interactive Communications

Interactive communications between government and citizens is the next step and is still at an embryonic stage. Santa Monica, California, is perhaps most advanced in the area of interactive communications so far. Many public policy issues such as care of the homeless, changes in zoning regulations and preservation of historic properties have been debated actively online. There are now about 4,000 users and that is increasing at the rate of about 100 per month. The system has two staff people, can receive 64 calls at once, and has a budget of about $100,000 per year.

Santa Monica City council members are online, as is their national congressional Representative, Mel Levine. Users and managers of the system feel that the public's opinions can be heard via this system, in a way not possible before.

The Cleveland Freenet system[5] has not yet enticed the local politicians online, but is the largest and most active of the interactive networks. It has 22,000 users (tripled in the past two years) with 4500-5000 log-ins per day. The system is free to users. Over 300 topics are monitored by volunteers and cover such things as medical advice provided by the Case Western University medical school staff, car repair service provided by various repair business owners, legal advice and many others. A conference topic can be set up by any individual or group that wants to manage and monitor it. Governmental information provided includes *Project Hermes*, which offers U.S. Supreme Court opinions within 20 minutes of a decision; *Campaign '90*, sponsored by the League of Women Voters, which puts position papers of candidates online along with biographies and candidates' statements. The winning candidates' statements stay online *forever* as a check on their performance. *Congressional Memory* summarizes the votes of U.S. Representatives from Ohio on national legislation.

The Freenet system is expanding to many other cities, including Cincinnati and Brexfield, Ohio and Peoria, Illinois. It is connecting with NetNorth (Canada) and Internet (colleges and universities) and Teleport (airports). Twelve or 13 more cities are scheduled to come online in the near future, including Helsinki, Singapore and cities in New Zealand.

Communicating With the Federal Government

There is little or no interactive online communication between U.S. Federal Governmental officials and their constituents. There is, of course, a great deal of use of new telecommunications technologies by the Federal government to gather, store and disseminate governmental information, and to manage their own information.

---

[5]Developed by Dr. Tom Grundner out of Case Western Reserve University, Cleveland, Ohio.

For example, the House of Representatives has an electronic information search system for its own use, electronic mail systems to District Offices, a survey service to sample constituent opinion, and uses video to transmit information to the media and to their constituents.

Representative Charlie Rose proposed a bill recently (H.R. 2772) that would establish in the Government Printing Office a single point of online public access to a wide range of Federal databases containing public information stored electronically. This is a first step in bringing people closer to their government and may eventually lead to the use of such systems for interactive discussion.

How Would a Public Forum Work?

The infrastructure of technologies needed for widespread interactive people/government networks is being developed and put in place now. The recent decision by Judge Greene, allowing the telephone companies to get into information dissemination services, will no doubt make a big difference in the rate of deployment. Suitable off-the-shelf computer hardware and software are available at moderate prices.

Computers are available in city halls, many schools, and in libraries. They could be installed in neighbourhood meeting places, hospitals, churches, movie theatres, etc.—wherever many people gather. A particularly successful interactive grassroots system began its operations out of a bar in Colorado Springs, Colorado. Interaction with government should be designed so that it is part of ordinary activities and not something that one has to go out of the way to do (as is going to a polling place, on a specified day, once every two or four years). It should also be part of an information system that is commonly used and commonly needed—the kinds of information being provided on the Cleveland Freenet and many radio talk shows (how do I fix my car, what's wrong with my elbow, where do I get a permit to remodel my house or sell my crafts, what are the local trash disposal regulations?).

"You cannot start to build consensus after a plan is developed. A process must be developed from the beginning which promotes cooperation amongst disparate interests in the economy."[6] Presenting a problem online with proposed changes or goals could be the first step in building consensus. Directions for response (limits of the problem, limits to proposed changes, where to write or call for additional information, and the timeframe for responses) should be made clear. Analyses of the public's proposed changes/ goals could then be presented for further online discussion. This could include impacts of the proposed changes on the economy, transportation systems, employment, individual rights, legal systems, etc. Implementing such a consensus-building system would require: consideration of implementation methods from the beginning; building institutions and networks; providing strong leadership; tapping available state and federal resources; carefully controlling expectations; and starting with small programs to build momentum for more involved strategies.[7]

A delphi survey technique could be used online to gather many opinions, summarize the viewpoints expressed, disseminate the summaries online and in local media, and repeat this process until it was felt a modicum of consensus on actions had been achieved.

The U.S. legal system has emphasized individual rights in the last 30 years. People have eagerly jumped onto that bandwagon. Now they need to be made more aware of community rights and their responsibilities to the community. Online discussions will facilitate that awareness by exposing them to the reasoning and feelings behind the demands of others.

---

[6]Cunningham, Keith, "Communities in Transition: Process for Adjustment Highlighted at Boston Conference,"*Nation's Cities Weekly,* November 11, 1991, p. 8. Mr. Cunningham is quoting Beth Siegel of Mt. Auburn Associates, a consultant to cities on strategic planning.
[7]Cunningham, op. cit.

The Role of Education and Training

While it is true now that "elites" have the most access to online systems, that will change in time. The telephone, the automobile and the television once were reserved for elites, and now are available to all strata of society. And just as those technologies broadened the world for all, so too will interactive computer systems broaden the world view of all by making accessible to them services, information and ideas not before encountered.

The next generation will not have to learn the difficult computer interfaces faced by today's adults. The interfaces are becoming more and more user friendly and eventually may reach the level of being operated with "plain English." Also, children are learning computer operations at very young ages now and in ten years computer literacy will be as widespread as telephone literacy is now.

The most important element in achieving meaningful citizen understanding of, and input to, governmental policy is education. Citizens need to be educated as to the responsibilities of government and, more importantly, as to their responsibilities as citizens and members of society.

Computers can be used in the schools (and other places) to teach people how to search for information, whether it be on governmental services, legislation or population demographics. Online conferencing can expose them to the fun and benefits of exchanging information with others, and of forming groups to push for reforms. Students could be formed into groups and given special projects involving focusing on some needed change in their school, neighbourhood, or local government. With an adviser, they would learn how to search for information, identify all the stakeholders involved in the chosen issue, identify those responsible for making change, develop alternative programs, and measure the costs and other ramifications of proposed changes. They also could be charged with trying to develop consensus by meeting with opposing factions, identifying their concerns and addressing those concerns or modifying their own demands in order to gain a consensus.

By going through this process, these students will gain a skill and knowledge that will be helpful to them throughout their lives, not only in dealing with government but in dealing with the many dilemmas faced in school, work, and at home. Their input to government will be reasonable and thoughtful, rather than the one-sided demands most often heard today.

Government's responsibility is not to "do all" for citizens, but it is their responsibility to manage the process and to show citizens how best to achieve their goals of good governance. New communications technologies can greatly aid in achieving this goal.